## October 7, 2003

## California Recalled its Governor for the First Time

**Governor Arnold Schwarzenegger on the day he surprised Jay Leno on the *Tonight Show* and told the world he was running for the office of governor.**

August 6, 2003 – Photo by Phil Dockter

**RECALL EDITION**

# California
## State & Local Government
# in Crisis

**5th Edition**

**Walt Huber - Glendale College**

"Hubie"
directs you to websites!

California State & Local Government In Crisis – 5th Edition
Copyright 2004, 2000, 1997, 1995, 1992
by Educational Textbook Company

**Educational Textbook Company**
P.O. Box 3597
Covina, California 91722
(626) 339-7733
FAX (626) 332-4744
www.etcbooks.com

All rights reserved. Printed in the United States of America. No part of this book may be reproduced or transmitted in any form or by any means, electronic or mechanical, including photocopying, recording, or any information storage and retrival system, without written permission from the Publisher.

Includes Index.

Library of Congress Cataloging in Publication Data

Huber, Walter Roy
California State & Local Government in Crisis

**ISBN #0-916772-56-X**

320.9794

1. California Politics and Government
2. Political Participation

I. Huber, Walter R., 1941  II. Title.

*Printed in California, U.S.A.*

# Preface

We constantly survey college professors to improve our reputation as the most up-to-date and comprehensive textbook on California politics. We'd like to thank the talented professors (many of whom were helpful in the writing of this book) who are dedicated to teaching college students about the workings of local and state government, and acknowledge them on the following pages.

You will find, throughout the text, editorials or current topics of discussion in rectangular boxes. We do express our personal opinions, but only in the editorial boxes.

The extensive index at the back of the book is specially designed to be student friendly. Also, you will enjoy the way that important vocabulary words are typeset in **BOLDFACE** type throughout the textbook and how easy-to-follow definitions are set in script. They cover any term that a first-time college student would need in a California state and local government course.

I want to express my appreciation to the following people whose contributions were invaluable to me in the writing of this book: Lance Widman of El Camino College, Dr. Owen Newcomer of Rio Hondo College, Tony Bernhard of University of California, Davis, Michael Newbrough, Ph.D., of Palomar College, Linda Serra, Andrea Adkins, Hasmik Sarkissian, and Eric Johnston of Glendale College, and Professor Bryan Reece of Cerritos College.

Special thanks also to Philip Dockter, art director; Rick Lee, layout and prepress, Colleen Taber, editor, and Linn Baker, proofreader.

My thanks to Carol and Chuck Dalool, who manage our office, and Professor Marcy Morris from Citrus College. Most of all, I thank our surveyed professors who set the standards for this effort to create a book designed for freshmen and sophomores.

**Walt Huber**

# Acknowledgements

**American River College**
  Tamir Sukkary
  Tressa Tabares

**Antelope Valley College**
  Donald R. Ranish

**Bakersfield College**
  C. Fivecoat
  Steven Holmes

**Cabrillo College**
  Gary Carlson

**Cal State Fullerton**
  Donald J. Matthewson

**Cerritos College**
  Thomas Sevener

**Chabot College**
  Chester D. Rhoan

**Chaffey College**
  Robert Melsh
  Monica Taylor

**Citrus College**
  F.C. VanWickle

**City College of San Francisco**
  Jo Ann Hendricks

**College of San Mateo**
  Leighton D. Armitage
  Joanne Roney Carpenter

**Compton College**
  Raymond Rodriguez

**Contra Costa College**
  Rocco C. Chavez
  Ted Radke

**Cosumnes River College**
  M. Morales

**Crafton Hills**
  Ken Cimino

**Cuyamaca College**
  Robert Holden

**Cypress College**
  Guinevere Hodges
  Peter Mathews

**De Anza College**
  James Hanley

**Diablo Valley College**
  V. W. Woolbright

**East Los Angeles College**
  Joel Busch

**Fresno City College**
  Brian McCully

**Glendale College**
  Andrea Adkins
  Linda Serra
  Eric K. Johnston
  Mark Weaver
  Hasmik Sarkissian

**Golden West College**
  Thomas A. Chambers

**Grossmont College**
  Adrienne Karel Leffler

**Imperial Valley College**
  Dr. Robert L. Wilhelm

**Laney College**
  Lawrence Saez

**Long Beach City College**
  John D. Chamberlain

**Los Angeles City College**
  Doyle Bates
  Ronald Pelton
  Philip J. Schlessinger

**Los Angeles Pierce College**
  Richard A. Moyer, Ph.D.

**L. A. Southwest College**
  Kerman Maddox

**L. A. Trade Tech. College**
  K. H. Theile, Ph.D.
  Gloria Hwang

**Los Angeles Valley College**
  Lawrence C. Jorgensen
  Richard Kazie

# Acknowledgements

**Los Medanos**
 Charles Bohakel

**Modesto College**
 Randy Siefkin

**Mt. San Antonio College**
 Henry Pacheco
 Leonard Shipman
 Maxine Sparks-Mackey

**Napa Valley College**
 Jean D. Schroeder

**Ohlone College**
 Howard A. Dewitt
 Alan Kirshner

**Orange Coast College**
 John Buckley
 Thomas Wert

**Palomar College**
 Warren Hawley
 Michael Newbrough, Ph.D.

**Palo Verde College**
 Kevin Eoff, Sr.

**Porterville College**
 G. R. Patterson

**Rio Hondo College**
 Owen Newcomer, Ph.D.

**Riverside Comm. College**
 Kristina Kauffman Cline

**Saddleback College**
 Tom Moody

**San Bernardino Valley College**
 Riase Jakpor, Ph.D.

**San Diego City College**
 Myles L. Clowers
 Donald H. Estes

**San Diego Mesa College**
 Sam H. Farahani, Ph.D.
 Carl Luna, Ph.D.
 Joe Mckenzie, Ph.D., JD.

**San Joaquin Delta College**
 Earnest Giannecchini

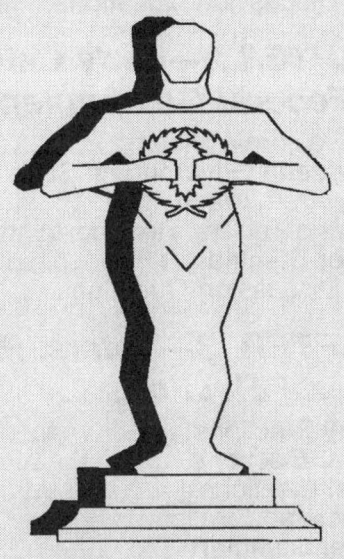

**Santa Barbara City College**
 John Kay
 D. Lawyer

**Santa Rosa College**
 W. R. Massey
 Gus P'manolis

**Skyline College**
 Johannes Masare

**Solano College**
 Jean Baxter

**Southwestern College**
 Alma Aguilar

**Ventura College**
 Kent Quinn

**West Hills College**
 Norine E. Oliver
 Raymond E. Smith

**West Los Angeles College**
 Jack D. Ruebensaal
 Mark Weaver

**Yuba College**
 David Rubiales

# Table of Contents

## CHAPTER 1—California In Crisis — 1
California's Growth Problem ......... 2
Facing California's Problems ......... 6
Facing California's Challenges ......... 11
California's Growing Economy ......... 13
Chapter Summary ......... 14
Class Discussion Questions ......... 15

## CHAPTER 2—Early California History and the Federal Government — 17
Early California History ......... 17
The Federal Government: State vs. Federal Powers ......... 29
Money From Washington ......... 31
State and Federal Reapportionment ......... 33
Chapter Summary ......... 34
Class Discussion Questions ......... 35

## CHAPTER 3—Voters, Primaries, and General Elections — 37
Primary Elections ......... 38
General Elections ......... 40
Special Elections ......... 41
Precincts and Ballots ......... 41
Chapter Summary ......... 45
Class Discussion Questions ......... 46

## CHAPTER 4—Direct Democracy — 49
The Father of California Direct Democracy ......... 49
Three Tools of Direct Democracy ......... 52
    The Recall ......... 52
    Referendum ......... 55
    Direct Initiative ......... 56
Chapter Summary ......... 58
Class Discussion Questions ......... 59

## CHAPTER 5—Interest Groups, Political Parties, and Campaigns — 61
Interest Groups ......... 61
Political Parties ......... 64
Campaigns ......... 68
Campaign Laws in California ......... 69
Chapter Summary ......... 72
Class Discussion Questions ......... 73

## CHAPTER 6—The Executive Branch — 77
Executive Branch ......... 77
The Office of Governor ......... 78

Administration of the Executive Branch.................................. 81
California's Plural Executive....................................................... 82
Recent Popular Governors......................................................... 85
Chapter Summary........................................................................ 88
Class Discussion Questions....................................................... 89

## CHAPTER 7—The California Legislature: Our Lawmakers          91

How the State Legislature Functions......................................... 91
California Senate......................................................................... 94
California Assembly.................................................................... 95
Committee System...................................................................... 96
Types of Legislation.................................................................... 98
Legislative Staff......................................................................... 100
Media Coverage........................................................................ 101
Chapter Summary..................................................................... 104
Class Discussion Questions.................................................... 105

## CHAPTER 8—Our Judicial System          107

California's Three-Level Court Structure................................ 108
Commissions and the Judicial Council................................... 111
Court Procedures...................................................................... 112
Attorneys and the State Bar..................................................... 114
Peace Officers........................................................................... 116
Citizens' Participation............................................................... 116
Chapter Summary..................................................................... 118
Class Discussion Questions.................................................... 119

## CHAPTER 9—Cities and Counties at the Crossroads          121

Counties..................................................................................... 122
Cities.......................................................................................... 126
Districts...................................................................................... 129
Regional Governance............................................................... 130
Chapter Summary..................................................................... 132
Class Discussion Questions.................................................... 134

## CHAPTER 10—Our State Budget Crisis          137

The California State Budget..................................................... 139
Types of State Taxes................................................................ 140
Spending: Where Taxes Go...................................................... 143
Bonds Mean Debt..................................................................... 146
Business Climate...................................................................... 146
Chapter Summary..................................................................... 149
Class Discussion Questions.................................................... 150

## Glossary          151
## Index          171

# California Facts

**State Capitals of California**

**San Jose:** November 13, 1849 to May 1, 1851
**Vallejo:** January 5, 1852 to February 4, 1853
(Temporarily in Sacramento January 16, 1852 to May 4, 1852)
**Benicia:** February 4, 1853 to February 25, 1854
**Sacramento:** February 25, 1854 to Present
**San Francisco:** January 24, 1862 to May 15, 1862 (Temporary)
**Sacramento:** 1869 Permanent Quarters

State Motto: "Eureka" (I have found it)
State Bird: California Quail (Lophortyx californica),
State Flower: California Golden Poppy (Eschsholtzia californica)
State Tree: California Redwood - the coast redwood (Sequoia sempervirens) and the giant sequoia (Sequoia gigantea)
State Reptile: the desert tortoise (Gopherus agassizi)
State Animal: California grizzly bear (Ursus californicus)
State Folk Dance: Square Dance
State Marine Fish: the garibaldi (Hypsypops rubicundus)
State Colors: Blue and Gold
State Marine Animal: the California gray whale (Eschrichtius robustus)
State Insect: The California dogface butterfly (Zerene eurydice)
State Mineral: Gold
State Rock: Serpentine
State Soil: The San Joaquin soil
State Gemstone: Benitoite
State Prehistoric Artifact: the chipped stone bear
State Fossil: The sabre-tooth cat (Smilodon californicus)
State Fish: The golden trout (Salmo agua-bonita)

State Dance: West coast swing dancing
State Theater: Pasadena Playhouse
State Fife & Drum Band: The California Consolidated Drum Band
State Song: "I Love You, California", written by F.B. Silverwood
Size: The third largest state, 163,707 square miles
Statehood: the 31st State. Admitted Sept. 9, 1850
Highest Point: Mt. Whitney at 14,494 feet above sea level
Lowest Point: Death Valley at 282 feet below sea level
Geographic Center of the State: 38 miles east of Madera
California's 1st Suspension Bridge, built in 1856, was relocated in Bidwell Canyon prior to the construction of the Oroville Dam.
Number of Counties: 58
Alpine, Mariposa, and Trinity counties—no incorporated cities within their borders.
Incorporated Cities in California: 477
Number of Chartered Cities: 105
Number of General Law Cities: 372
Total Area: 163,707 square miles
Total Land Area: 155,973 square miles
Total Water Area: 7,734 square miles
Shoreline: 3,427 miles
Coastline: 840 miles

Figures as of June 2001

# Chapter 1
# California in Crisis

## CALIFORNIA: THE GROWING BUDGET CRISIS!

Actor and businessman Arnold Schwarzenegger won the first successful recall election in California history. Former Governor Gray Davis was expelled from office due to the voters' perception that he mismanaged California's finances. The 2003 California budget was passed by the legislature and signed by Gray Davis just as the governor's recall petition signatures were about to be submitted.

The skyrocketing state budget deficit (loss) had become so huge that there was no money left to pay bills. Because the state government cannot, by law, carry a deficit, the Davis administration chose to borrow huge sums of money (bonds), thereby mortgaging the future of California. The continual issuing of bonds forced the state's bond rating to become the worst in the nation and the bond interest rates to be the highest. There will continue to be overspending until the state Budget Crisis is solved.

The "California Budget Crisis" should more accurately be called the "California Deficit Crisis," because our ex-governor and the legislature consistently spent a lot more than money than the state had. They justified spending that exceeded the state's revenue (income) by blaming it on the dot.com crash, among other things. Their slow reaction to our so-called "electricity crisis," resulting in expensive, fixed, long-term contracts, also added huge costs to the budget.

Irresponsible over-spending committed California to high operating costs for years. Governor Schwarzenegger inherited, at the minimum, an $8 billion deficit. Fulfilling his campaign promise to repeal the 300% increase in auto registration fees means another $4 billion added to the deficit. The state's budget will take many more years to straighten out. See Chapter 10 for a more detailed explanation of the state's revenue and expenses.

**Chapter 1**

## CALIFORNIA: BUSINESS SECTOR IS GROWING

California business is slowly experiencing the next economic upswing. But, as the economy grows so do job opportunities and salaries, drawing more and more people to the state, and straining an already overburdened infrastructure. With our current population, our highways are congested, housing costs are rising, healthcare and public services for the poor are grossly inadequate, the quality of our air and water continues to suffer, and our public schools remain understaffed and overcrowded.

Governor Arnold Schwarzenegger is focused on changing California by bringing us out of the most anti-business legislative environment in decades. The fact is, high state taxes and excessive regulations are responsible for some corporations (who pay the most taxes) relocating operations out of state. But with a business-friendly governor in office, the future of business is looking up once again.

## *California's Growth Problem*

www.dof.ca.gov
**California Department of Finance**

### ABOUT GROWTH

> **FACT:** California has 12.3% of the nation's population! It is projected to be 12.8% by 2010.

### POPULATION: KEEPS GROWING AND GROWING

> **FACT:** Every 24 hours, California's population increases by 1,644; most are immigrants or children of immigrants.

The fact is, California's population is growing rapidly because of our easily accessible borders, economic opportunities unmatched by other states or nations, and recent immigrants, who tend to have relatively high birth rates.

The "Golden State" should really be called the "growth state" even though projected growth will be less, on a percentage basis, than in past decades. California's growth rate will be close to double the national rate.

The last census indicated that one out of eight U.S. residents lives in California. In the decades ahead, one-fourth of the U.S. population growth will occur in California.

## *California in Crisis*

### CALIFORNIA
### Strong Growth Projections

|  | 2000 | 2010 | California % Change | U.S. % Change |
|---|---|---|---|---|
| Jobs | 16.2 million | 19.0 million | 17.8% | 11.6% |
| Income | $1.1 trillion | $1.6 trillion | 40.8 | 33.5 |
| Households | 11.5 million | 13.2 million | 15.3 | 11.4 |
| Population | 34.0 million | 39.7 million | 17.2 | 10.0 |

 www.ccsce.com

Center for Continuing Study of the California Economy
—Stephen Levy, California's preeminent statistical authority.

## JOBS DRAW PEOPLE TO CALIFORNIA

**FACT:** The state's population keeps growing because the number of jobs in California keeps growing.

Jobs are still the primary factor encouraging people to migrate and immigrate here. People come for these jobs despite high housing prices, congested highways, and environmental problems. Look at the above chart: California is growing faster than the nation.

## CALIFORNIA OUTPACES THE NATION

**FACT:** In the next decade, California will outpace the nation in jobs, income, household, and population growth.

Because it is virtually impossible to slow population growth in the state, California's biggest challenge will be how to make room for its yearly increase of over 600,000 people. In 2004, California's population reached 35.5 million.

## CALIFORNIA'S FUTURE GROWTH SECTORS:

1. High Technology
2. Foreign Trade
3. Tourism and Entertainment
4. Professional Services
5. Diversified Manufacturing

**Chapter 1**

## REGIONAL PROJECTIONS

**LOS ANGELES BASIN** – Los Angeles accounts for nearly half of the state's jobs and population (17.3 million residents). The region has a diverse and strong economic base built around the country's largest port complex, largest entertainment and tourism industry, largest diversified manufacturing center and participation in the fast-growing professional services, bio-tech and design markets. The aerospace industry is expected to turn around as well, with defense technology spending once again on the rise.

**SAN FRANCISCO BAY AREA** – The Bay Area has gone from one of the leaders in job and income growth to one that lags behind other regions, due mainly to the bursting of the dot.com bubble. The economy is expected to turn around eventually, with rising profits, faster U.S. economy growth, and a recovery in sales of technology goods and services. There is very little land left on which to build, so housing prices continue to be higher than the rest of the state.

**SAN DIEGO** – Being adjacent to the Mexican border, San Diego is considered one of the fastest growing foreign trade sectors in the nation. World-class university research programs, Scripp's Research Institute's leadership in biotechnology, a broad base in technology, and developing telecommunications industries, as well as a healthy tourism business, bode well for the region's economy. San Diego is expected to continue to be one of the fastest growing regions in California and the nation in terms of income and spending growth.

**SACRAMENTO** – Central to state government in California, professional services related to state government have become a high-growth sector. A major distribution center on the I-80 corridor, Sacramento continues to attract high-tech firms like Oracle, EDS, and TASQ Technology to the area. The new professional, scientific, technical, and management services sector is the fastest growing part of the region's economic base. Job growth projections that are higher than both the state and the nation, the availability of moderately-priced homes, and the proximity to Silicon Valley means the population will continue growing rapidly.

**SAN JOAQUIN VALLEY** – The Valley is seeing tremendous new residential housing growth and an increase in population-serving jobs. The region expects to outpace the state and nation in job growth to 2010, but will need to attract new basic industry jobs to replace slow-growing farm activity (which is still the largest single industry in the Valley). Marginal farmland will be replaced by affordable housing as the number of farm jobs continues to decrease in the years ahead. The new UC campus at Merced is expected to attract start-up industrial and technology developments, particularly in agricultural products—like innovative food packaging.

*California in Crisis*

# California's Ethnic Diversity

Racial and ethnic population - 2000 Census.

### ASIANS     California
**CENSUS 2000**

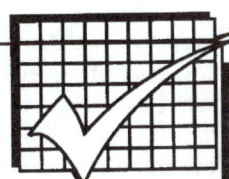

| | |
|---|---|
| Filipino | 1,098,321 |
| Chinese | 1,122,187 |
| Japanese | 394,896 |
| Vietnamese | 484,023 |
| Korean | 375,571 |
| Indian | 360,392 |
| Laotian, Cambodian, Thai | 196,485 |
| Hmong | 71,741 |
| All others | 85,110 |

### PACIFIC ISLANDERS

| | |
|---|---|
| Hawaiian | 60,048 |
| Samoan | 49,804 |
| Guamanian or Chamorro | 33,849 |
| Tongan | 15,252 |

### HISPANICS

| | |
|---|---|
| Mexican | 8,455,926 |
| Puerto Rican | 140,570 |
| Cuban | 72,286 |
| All Others Combined | 2,297,774 |

(census did not break others down)

### ETHNIC BREAKDOWN

| | |
|---|---|
| WHITE (NON-HISPANIC) - 46.7% | 15.8 million |
| BLACK, (AFRO-AMERICAN) - 6.4% | 2.2 million |
| HISPANIC - 32.4% | 11 million |
| ASIAN - 10.9% | 3.7 million |
| Other - 3.7% | 1.2 million |
| CALIFORNIA | 33.9 million |

### *CALIFORNIA (Projections 2010) 39.7 million*

WHITE (NON-HISPANIC) - **46%**
BLACK, (AFRO-AMERICAN) - **7%**
HISPANIC - **36%**
ASIAN and Other - **11%**

**Chapter 1**

These are California's high-growth sectors for the next decade. Focus your attention on these sectors because they are growing faster than the U. S. economy.

New products and technologies in multimedia, advanced telecommunications, and the use of the Internet symbolize the state's leadership position in future growth industries. California already has the economic base that other regions and nations are striving to create.

## CALIFORNIA'S GROWING ETHNIC DIVERSITY

> **FACT:** There is no single majority group in California. Today over 50% of all Californians are Asian, Black, or Hispanic.

About one-half of our population growth in the last decade was due to immigration from other countries. The other half was due to births exceeding deaths. Overall, about 75% of the growth in the last decade occurred among Hispanics, Blacks, and Asians. Hispanics are the largest growing group, but Asians are the fastest growing group in California, by percentage.

# Facing California's Problems

## K-12 EDUCATION IS STILL SUFFERING

> **FACT:** To keep up with current population explosion, California still needs to build new classrooms or remodel old schools.

Kindergarten through 12th grade education has suffered because of California's continuing growth. There are so many students that education is the single largest expense for our state and county governments. Even though California has increased its educational spending to 42% of the state's annual budget, we still only rank 30th in the nation in per-child education spending.

There will be no slowdown predicted for the increasing number of school children before the year 2007. Until then, students' growth will exacerbate the existing problem of demand for classrooms, textbooks, and teachers.

Unlike most other countries that require excellence in K-12 grades, we also demand excellence in college work and create opportunities for anyone who wants to attend college. Our downfall is that many students fall through the cracks in the K-12 grades and are not prepared to go on to college. At this time, our system does not provide good vocational alternatives for such students.

# Schools Down – Colleges Up
# K-12 Enrollment
# (K-12 to Peak in 2008, fall by 2011)

**School Enrollment Dropping**

California, the growth state, is beginning to experience a dramatic reversal in educational enrollment trends, after decades of constant and huge Kindergarten-12th grade (K-12) enrollment increases. These students are are now moving on to college and older students are coming back for retraining.

Projections show K-12 enrollment peaking in the 2007-2008 school year. By 2011, the K-12 enrollment growth rate will be 0% or drop slightly. We will stop building new K-12 schools but continue to build new colleges. Enrollment figures suggest migration rates to other states, new immigrant rates, and birth rates will remain steady.

**Fact: K-12 enrollment rates will decline until 2008, then level off.**

The key is to balance new construction and renovation of schools, keeping in mind projected enrollment declines ahead. A new approach would be to start combining school and community facilities so building funds could be utilized for both.

Since Proposition 98 mandates that 40% of the general fund budget must go K-12 and community colleges, educational funds will probably be allocated more to community colleges.

## CALIFORNIA ENROLLMENT TRENDS
### 1990-2011 (Thousands)

|  | 1990 | 2001 | 2011 | Percent Change 2001-2011 |
|---|---|---|---|---|
| K-12 | 4,842.2 | 6,068.9 | 6,295.3 | 3.7% |
| Community Colleges | 1,513.0 | 1,686.6 | 2,090.1 | 23.9% |
| UC, CSU | 522.7 | 567.6 | 751.4 | 32.4% |
| Higher Education (All) | 2,035.7 | 2,254.2 | 2,841.5 | 26.0% |

Source: California Department of Finance

*Chapter 1*

### College Enrollment Increasing

California's public higher education system, the California Community Colleges (CCC), California State University (CSU), and the University of California (UC), will grow from a total of 2.3 million full-time students to more than 2.8 million in 2011.

**Fact: California Community Colleges (CCC) Account for 75% of all College Students.**

As a result, community colleges will see by far the largest numerical enrollment gains. But as a percentage, UC and CSU enrollment gains will be higher.

California's public colleges make us economically competitive; this is a major plus for our state. The key is to make sure the governor and the legislature keep access to these higher education institutions affordable to California residents.

Source: California Department of Finance

### HIGHER EDUCATION IS EXCELLENT

In California, we hear a lot about our K-12 schools struggling for more money, increased space, better high school graduation rates, and higher achievement scores, but this certainly does not apply to California's colleges.

California colleges are not only the envy of the United States, but also the rest of the world, which sends its sons and daughters to study here.

There are over 108 community colleges in California with enrollment of well over a million students. This constitutes about 20% of America's community colleges. Our California State University (CSU) and University of California (UC) systems are highly ranked and still relatively inexpensive, even to nonresidents.

Even with increases in tuition, higher education is still a bargain in California. Community colleges, state colleges, and universities have the largest number students enrolled in the nation.

## California in Crisis

### EVEN OUR PRISONS ARE OVERCROWDED

**FACT:** California has over 161,000 convicts in its prisons.

California's state prison system is dangerously overcrowded, with no relief in sight. The increasing cost and overcrowding renews the old debate about what is the best way to deal with crime and punishment in this state. The "Three Strikes Law" has cost millions in additional housing expenses and new prisons. Reformers say there must be a better and cheaper way, while at the same time hard-liners feel that we are not strict enough. The cost of keeping a prisoner incarcerated for a year is over $34,000. Hard-liners argue that the cost to society would be far greater if criminals were left out on the streets. The cost of running prisons, including large overtime pay increases to prison guards, has dramatically increased. Could the large contributions to former Governor Gray Davis's campaign have influenced his negotiations with the prison guards' union?

### BETTER TRANSPORTATION IS NEEDED

**FACT:** Each day there are 1,000 more cars on our roads.

Until recently, when California voters agreed to double their gasoline taxes for transportation, there seemed to be no public interest for decades in lowering the freeway travel time. In addition, voters have approved two propositions that require the issuance of billions of dollars in bonds just to improve our crumbling transportation system. This is one area where California stepped forward to become a better state by accepting the challenge of improving its crowded roads.

Extending freeway shoulders to add additional lanes, without purchasing new land, and building new expensive freeway foundations, has been a blessing. This has been a simple way to increase the flow of traffic on our freeways. But now that these inexpensive ways to ease traffic have been used, how do we reduce traffic in the future?

### AIR QUALITY

Smog, the long-time air problem of Los Angeles, has spread over a large portion of Southern California. With 1,000 more cars on the road each day due to California's increasing population, it is no wonder that the southern part of the state has serious air quality problems. The cherished car is causing most of the problems. Organizations with over 100 employees must regulate hours, encourage car pooling, and utilize electric cars, according to the Air Quality Management District (AQMD).

Chapter 1

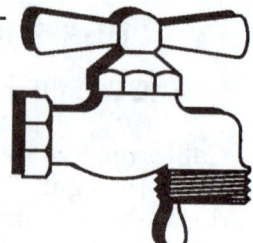

## California's Most Precious Resource ...Water

1. Continuous water shortages
2. Ground water pollution
3. Environmental concerns in Mono basin
4. Arizona is taking more Colorado River water
5. Erratic weather patterns (drought/flood)

Water wars in the past have pitted: Northern California vs. Southern California, San Diego vs. Los Angeles, and Consumer vs. Agriculture.

Some water experts say that the key for Southern California is to expand its reservoir system (like the new Diamond Valley Lake in Southern California) to allow storage of more water during wet years. In drought years, mandatory water rationing would be required and water conservation would be encouraged at all times. If all else fails, we can try desalinization of the Pacific Ocean.

The AQMD's new strategy is to reduce microscopic pollutants, which consist primarily of road dust. Cities and counties can reduce the gritty, gray haze found in the Los Angeles basin by controlling dust from unpaved roads and by improved street cleaning.

## WASTE MANAGEMENT AND LANDFILLS

Landfill sites in California are filling up fast. As local landfill sites reach their limits, more costly sites must be opened even further from major cities. Recycling has reduced the amount of trash per individual, but the number of individuals is increasing so fast that we take one step back for every two forward.

The waste management problem will reach a crisis stage in about a decade when most of Southern California's urban dumps will be filled. That is when trash hauling by train will likely be the most common way of disposal. Cities today pay between $11 and $33 a ton to get rid of their trash. But higher transportation costs, as well as tougher landfill requirements, will soon double this expense. It looks like $50 a ton to dispose of trash will soon seem like a bargain.

## HOUSING PROBLEM (CALIFORNIA'S HIGH COST)

Home prices continue to increase, averaging 5-10% a year. As jobs, income, population, and households increase, fewer people will be able to afford to buy property. Less than 40% of Californians own their own homes, since the median selling price of a house is over $400,000. One-third of owners and one-half of renters in California are paying 30% or more of their income for housing.

> **FACT:** Californians must build 550 apartment units, condos, or homes each day to meet continuous growth.

With so many new people arriving or being born each day in California, it is no wonder that real estate prices remain high.

The secret of owning a house, "the American Dream," is to start off small. Starter properties, usually found in outer suburbs, include smaller condos, or are in lower income areas. No income taxes have to be paid on the first $250,000 of gain when you sell your home if you are single and the first $500,000 if you are married.

## Facing California's Challenges

> **FACT:** A yearly average increase of 600,000 in California's population is projected between 2000-2010.

It may seem strange to talk at length about California's problems when we lead the nation in economic growth. However, our population growth and growing ethnic diversity are forcing voters to increasingly make urgent and sometimes painful political decisions to ease the state's growing pains. Politicians continue to face challenges resulting from California's increasing population growth.

### THE POPULATION GROWTH CHALLENGE

Handling California's growing population and the problems it creates is our number one challenge. There must be a change in the state's priorities, including tax structure and spending options, to deal with the massive population growth that will continue into the next decade. The real challenge is not how to stop growth but to find ways to slow growth down.

How our state responds to these problems will determine the future of California. Our politics, like all politics, is the process of arriving at a consensus on how the state is to be governed. In a democratic form of government, our elected officials decide what our laws should be, and how our laws are written, base, at least in theory, on the will of the people.

### Chapter 1

## THE PRODUCTIVITY CHALLENGE

Increasing productivity is the key to raising our standard of living. *PRODUCTIVITY is the ability to produce an amount of goods and services per working hour.* With the expansion of the Internet and computer software (most of which is created right here in California), companies and individuals are capable of doing more in less time. In our new global economy, the country, state, firm, or individual that is more productive will be the one that moves ahead. The concept is simple: accomplish more during the hours you work. By utilizing improved communication technologies, it is not necessary to work harder but to work smarter.

If our federal and state governments would encourage (1) more money to be invested in new equipment and state-of-the-art technology and (2) better education for our students and workers, our economy would be more productive!

## THE CULTURAL DIVERSITY CHALLENGE

California's incredible ethnic diversity poses one of our biggest challenges. If you look at the census breakdown, you can see the wide-range of cultures represented in the state. Each group has special needs and concerns. The political dilemma facing the government is how to provide services for each diverse group and, at the same time, not raise taxes beyond what is already one of the highest levels in the country.

## LEGISLATURE TOO ANTI-BUSINESS

**"California is the 49th-ranked state in business climate."**

Before his recall, Governor Gray Davis and the state legislature headed up the most "anti-business" administration ever. Pro-union and anti-business sentiment only served to hurt employers, employees, and the California economy. One reason a state with so many advantages suffered such a large negative economic decline was because of bad government decisions made over a number of years.

**"California used to be one of the worst places in the United States in which to do business."**

Although the leader in so many business arenas, like high-technology, foreign trade, tourism and entertainment, professional services, and diversified manufacturing, the state could not withstand the assault of so much anti-business legislation for long. Some of those regulations resulted in:

*California in Crisis*

## How Big is California's Economy?

1. U.S. – $10,171 BILLION
2. JAPAN – $4,245 BILLION
3. GERMANY – $1,874 BILLION
4. UNITED KINGDOM – $1,406 BILLION
5. **CALIFORNIA – $1,392 BILLION**
6. FRANCE – $1,303 BILLION
7. CHINA – $1,159 BILLION
8. ITALY – $1.091 BILLION
9. CANADA – $677 BILLION
10. MEXICO – $618 BILLION
11. SPAIN – $577 BILLION

**Although not a country, California still has the 5th largest economy the world!**

1. The second highest personal income tax rate in the nation.
2. One of the highest corporate tax rates in the nation.
3. The second highest electricity rates in the nation.
4. Overly complex, costly, and time-consuming business regulations.
5. One of the worst workers' compensation systems in the nation.
6. Sales taxes well above the national average.
7. 50th in spending per capita on highways.
8. Overdue water projects.
9. Inadequate school facilities.
10. 32% higher cost of unemployment insurance.

## THE CALIFORNIA BUSINESS CHALLENGE

California businesses are among the most regulated and taxed in the nation. If a business feels that it can make larger profits in the long-run by moving out of state, it will do so.

## *California's Growing Economy*

**FACT:** California handles over 21.5% of all U.S. trade.

Trade is clearly one of the driving industries in California. Between exports and imports, California has boosted jobs in air transportation, wholesale trades, and port facilities. Our state is outperforming the nation in exports

**Chapter 1**

because: 1) our major trading partners have above average economic growth and 2) our exports are concentrated in high growth industries.

***EXPORTS*** *are manufactured goods, agricultural produce, minerals, and other items produced in the United States but purchased by other countries.* Our top seven export partners are: Mexico, Japan, Canada, Taiwan, South Korea, United Kingdom, and China. ***IMPORTS*** *are goods and services purchased from other countries.*

## CALIFORNIA: A WORLD CLASS ECONOMIC POWER

**FACT:** California ranks 5th in world economic power!

California is a world class economic power because it is economically diverse. ***ECONOMIC DIVERSITY*** *means that many economic activities are balanced so that no one industry dominates to the extent that, if eliminated, it would cause severe problems.* Economic power is measured by gross domestic product. ***GROSS DOMESTIC PRODUCT (GDP)*** *is the sum of all products and services produced by a country in a given year.*

## Chapter Summary

Official Census figures can be misleading, as they notoriously undercount minorities. According to more realistic sources, it's estimated that Hispanics make up 32.4% of our population, and statistically have the most children. Blacks and whites have a more static birthrate, with blacks comprising 6.4% of the state population. Whites make up the largest single group, 46.7%, Asians make up an additional 10.8%, and all others combine for 3.7%. Currently about half our population is considered "non-white."

California's economy is being led by our future growth sectors:

1. foreign trade,
2. bio- and high-tech,
3. tourism and entertainment,
4. professional services, and
5. diversified manufacturing.

Public education is the state's single largest budget item. No matter how much money we spend, we can't seem to keep pace with the growing number of students. But after 2007, our student population growth rate will level off and start to decline.

## California in Crisis

Every day in California there are another 1,000 automobiles on the roads. New roads and freeways must be built, and the present system must be maintained and earthquake-proofed.

Our prisons are also terribly overcrowded. We currently have over 161,000 people in our prison system.

Trash disposal is also reaching a crisis point. Our landfills are filling up quickly. Because water is a precious commodity in California, we have had to buy up water rights elsewhere and build an expensive system of aqueducts to keep our thirsty southland supplied. Conservation, recycling, and desalinization are all being attempted. Needless to say, these solutions will cost money.

One answer to this crisis is a renewed focus on productivity. By investing more in education, new technologies, and by lifting unnecessary regulations and excessive taxes, we can make California a more viable place for companies to do business. California has the fifth largest economy on earth. We are America's gateway to the huge manufacturing centers of the Pacific Rim and Mexico. Trade will be essential to our future. The challenge is to improve the business climate without damaging the quality of life our citizens have come to expect. If we encourage progressive companies to make California their home, the crisis of today could become the economic triumph of tomorrow.

### Class Discussion Questions

1. What brings so many people to California?

2. What effects does cultural diversity have on California?

3. Are California's problems and challenges overwhelming, or do you think we can overcome them? How?

4. How can we reduce overcrowding in the prison system?

5. How can California attract and keep businesses?

# Chapter 2
# Early California History and the Federal Government

www.ca.gov/s/history (state site)
www.museumca.org/goldrush (museum)
www.calgoldrush.com (Sacramento Bee)
www.sfmuseum.org (museum)

## Early California History

### NATIVE AMERICANS

Native Americans numbered about 150,000 before the Europeans started coming in large numbers to California. The moderate climate and abundant food supply sustained the 135 loosely organized tribes. At one time one-eighth of all indigenous Indian Tribes lived in California.

The white man greatly contributed to the decline of the Indian population through the introduction of diseases (small pox, malaria, venereal disease), manufactured Indian wars, and the destruction of their food supplies. By 1900 there were only about 16,000 Native Americans remaining in California.

### UNDER THE FLAG OF SPAIN

In 1542, on a voyage paralleling the California coast, Juan Rodriquez Cabrillo sailed into San Diego Bay and named it "San Miguel." Although the name did not survive, Cabrillo is credited with being the first European to land in what is now known as California. The Spanish established settlements along the California coastline. These settlements were linked when the mission system was created.

Chapter 2

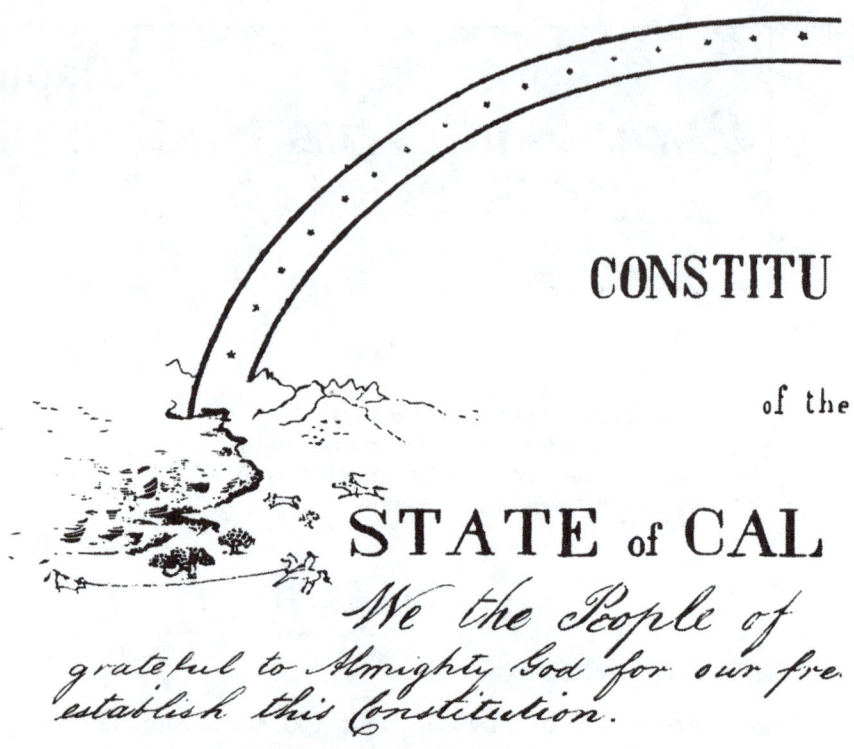

## California's Political/Historical Timeline
### SUMMARY OF IMPORTANT HISTORICAL DATES

**1500** – Native Indians who first inhabited the land numbered 150,000 before the white man introduced his diseases and prejudice.

**1542** – Juan Rodriguez Cabrillo discovered San Diego—the first European to set foot in California—only 50 years after Columbus discovered "America."

**1769** – Father Junipero Serra began establishing the first of 21 Missions from San Diego to Sonoma, each a one-day horseback ride apart.

**1821** – Mexico won its independence from Spain in 1821.

**1827** – Jedediah Smith, the first American to cross the Sierra Mountains, arrived in California.

**1848** – Gold was discovered by James Marshall near Sacramento at Sutter's sawmill. "Eureka" (I have found it) – the gold rush was on.

**1848** – Treaty of Guadalupe Hidalgo – Mexico officially ceded California to the United States.

**1849** – California's first constitution.

# Early California History and the Federal Government

**1850** – California is admitted to the Union as the 31st state on September 9, 1850.

**1869** – Transcontinental railroad completed – The Southern Pacific Railroad continued its growth and monopolistic practices; later it became known as the "Octopus."

**1880** – California adopted its second constitution, restricting Chinese employment, railroads, and corporate officials.

**1911** – An amendment to the State Constitution gave us the tools of direct democracy. recall, referendum, and initiative.

**1942** – Beginning of internment during World II of Japanese-American citizens.

**1978** – Proposition 13 passed by voters. This property tax limitation initiative helped overtaxed homeowners, but greatly restricted county government.

**1988** – Proposition 98 mandated that at least 40% of general funds must go to K-12 and community colleges.

**1990** – Proposition 140 passed. This term limitation initiative reduced the number of terms that a state legislator could serve and lessened their staffs and pensions.

**1994** – Proposition 187 limited public services that could be offered to illegal aliens.

**2003** – For the first time, California recalled its governor, Gray Davis.

**2003** – Arnold Schwarzenegger became governor.

# Chapter 2

## CALIFORNIA MISSIONS

Father Junipero Serra is recognized as the first real colonizer of California. Father Serra, a Catholic Franciscan Priest from Spain, established the first mission (1769) near what is now downtown San Diego. The second mission, near Monterey Bay, is where Father Serra is buried. Spain used four types of settlements to colonize California: missions, presidios, pueblos, and ranchos.

The *MISSIONS were Spanish style adobe buildings with high arches, long corridors, and red tiled roofs that surrounded a courtyard.* Missions were created for more than religious instruction. They were similar to vocational schools where the natives could learn a trade and how to care for farms and orchards. Father Serra personally established nine missions, the number later growing to 21.

*PRESIDIOS were frontier forts.* Most were located at strategic locations, usually at the entrance to a pueblo or port. *PUEBLOS were clusters of adobe houses, usually including a church, that formed a town or small city.* Among the first settlements were San Jose in 1777 and Los Angeles, "the City of the Angels," in 1781.

*EL CAMINO REAL is Spanish for "The King's Highway."* It is the original horseback trail used to travel between missions and from presidio to presidio. The missions were located so that they were only a day's horseback ride from each other. Bells on a staff-shaped post now mark these routes and are often seen on US Route 1 while traveling along the California coast.

## MEXICAN RULE 1821 - 1846

Mexico won its independence from Spain in 1821.

**Historical note:** Mexico repelled a French invasion force on May 5, 1862. *CINCO de MAYO (The fifth of May) marks the date of the battle with the French in which Mexico turned back its first foreign invader as an independent country.* Cinco de Mayo is more widely celebrated here than is Mexico's independence from Spain.

In 1833, under the Mexican Secularization Act, Mexico seized the missions and the surrounding lands. They then distributed half the land to the California Indians. The missions were stripped of their lands and converted into parish churches.

# Early California History and the Federal Government

At the same time, some select, wealthy gentlemen established ranchos. The *RANCHOS were large parcels of land given to families of prominence to establish large, un-fenced grazing areas for raising cattle.* Between 1830 and 1845, the number of private ranchos on land grants increased from 50 to 1,045.

## CALIFORNIA IS TAKEN FROM MEXICO

The Bear Flag Revolt started in California on June 14, 1846, before anyone realized that the United States had already declared war on Mexico. The *BEAR FLAG REVOLT started over the fear that the Mexican government would move against settlers in California.* The revolt began in Sonoma where General Marino Guadalupe Vallejo was put under house arrest by a band of American settlers who declared an independent "Republic of California." A symbol of this battle was a flag with a bear gazing at a single star. The motto on the flag read:

> **"A bear stands his ground always, and as long as the stars shine we stand for the cause."**

The Bear Flag Revolt was a short-lived event. It ended 22 days later when Mexico surrendered control of Monterey to U.S. forces.

**EARLY FLAG**

**Chapter 2**

The United States had declared war on Mexico in 1846 over a boundary dispute in Texas. By 1847, U.S. Troops had control of Texas, New Mexico, Arizona, and California. The United States and Mexico signed the Treaty of Guadalupe Hidalgo on February 2, 1848. The *TREATY OF GUADALUPE HIDALGO ended the war with Mexico and allowed the California Republic to become part of the United States.* The treaty honored the earlier Spanish land grants and later Mexican land grants.

**CURRENT FLAG**

## GOLD WAS DISCOVERED

On January 24, 1848, gold was discovered by James Wilson Marshall, a carpenter employed by John Sutter to construct a sawmill at Coloma on a branch of the American River. The sound of "Eureka!" was heard around the world. EUREKA refers to the gold rush and means "I have found it!"

The greatest influx of gold hunters was in 1849, hence the new arrivals were given the name "forty-niners." Hysteria about the amount of gold caused California's population to swell, especially around Sacramento, from 15,000 in 1848, to over 92,000 by 1850 and again to 380,000 by 1860. But even after the gold fever broke, people continued to come. The completion of the transcontinental railroad (1869) continued to bring more people to establish or work in merchandising and manufacturing companies.

# Early California History and the Federal Government

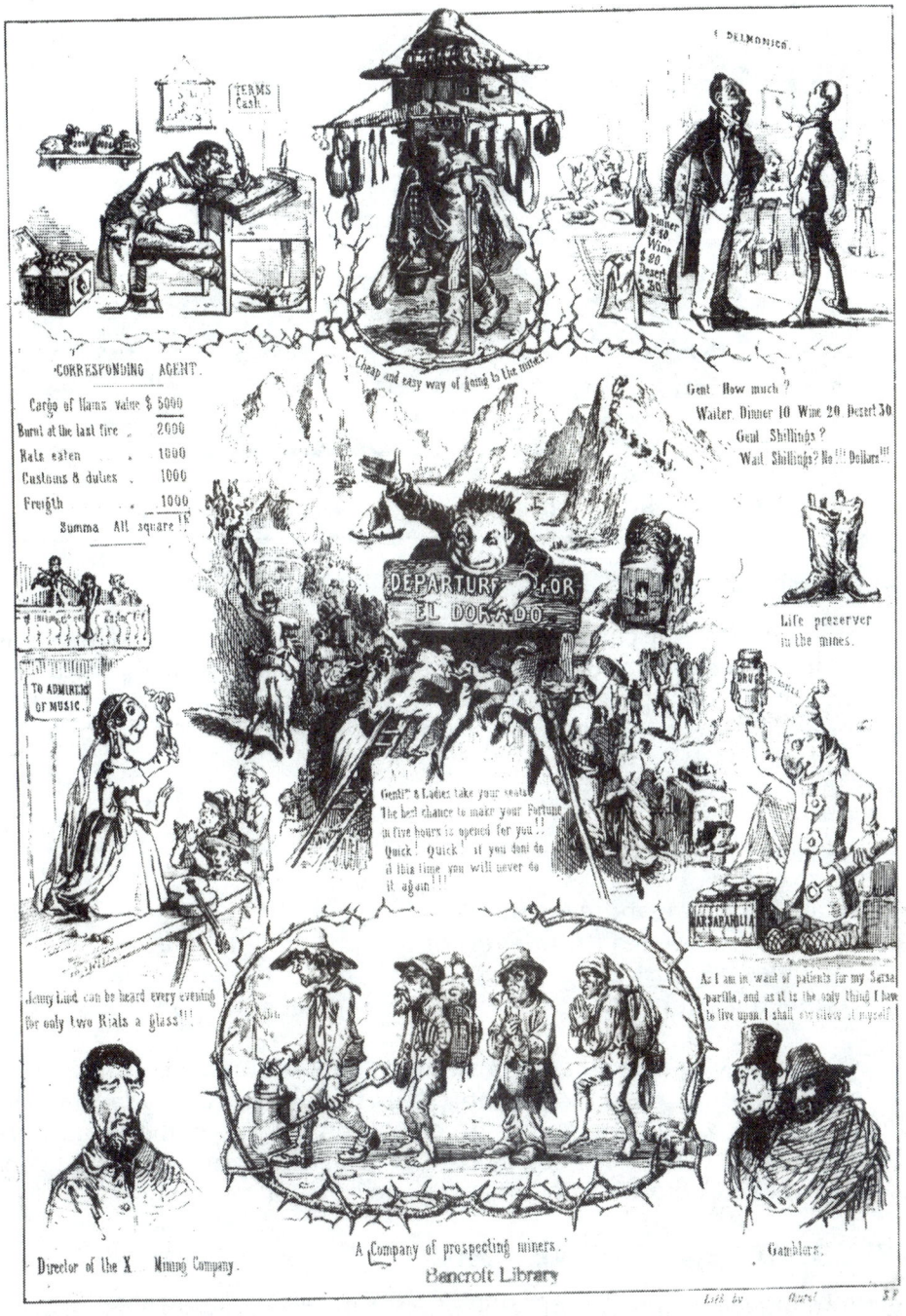

Chapter 2

Engraved by Charles H. Holmes, of Sacramento, in 1888; copied from an old print in an early California magazine.

**California Capitol Building at San Jose — 1849-1851**

## CALIFORNIA STATEHOOD 1850

In the Fall of 1849, a constitutional convention was held, and the new Californians overwhelmingly approved their first California Constitution. It established a state government that is similar to today's state government.

The California constitution included:

    Bill of Rights (in the beginning)
    Plural executive branch
    Legislature (Senate and Assembly)
    Elected judicial branch (four levels of courts—now three levels)
    White males 21 years of age could vote
    Government documents were printed in English and Spanish.

The U.S. Congress approved this constitution and California became the 31st state admitted to the Union. *ADMISSION DAY is September 9, 1850, the date California became a state.* There was much concern as to whether California would be admitted as a slave or free state, but the U.S. Congress moved very quickly to make California another non-slave state for the Union.

## THE GREAT SEAL OF CALIFORNIA

The constitutional convention of 1849 adopted the "Great Seal of the State of California." Around the top of the ring are 31 stars representing California's

# Early California History and the Federal Government

position as the 31st state admitted to the Union. The foreground figure represents the Goddess Minerva who, according to Greek mythology, sprang full-grown from the head of Zeus, her father. She symbolizes the political birth of the state of California without having to go through the probation of being a territory. At her feet is a gold miner and also a grizzly bear feeding on grape vines. The snow-capped peaks of the Sierra Nevada are in the background with the state motto "Eureka," which refers to the gold rush.

The Secretary of State is the keeper of the Great Seal, which is used to emboss official state documents. A person who misuses or reproduces the Great Seal without permission is guilty of a misdemeanor.

## THE RAILROADS (GOOD AND BAD)

The Central Pacific Railroad Company's eventual founders were referred to as the "Big Four." Their last names may still sound familiar today:

**Leland Stanford**
**Collis P. Huntington**
**Mark Hopkins**
**Charles Crocker**

President Lincoln signed the Pacific Railroad Bill (1862) that called for the simultaneous start of the Central Pacific Railroad in Sacramento and Union Pacific Railroad in Omaha. The bill called for these two railroad lines to receive land and government subsidies based on the miles of rail laid. The extreme wealth and power of the big four railroad barons enabled them to gain a stranglehold on the early economic and political life of California. For 50 years (1860-1910), the railroads were the dominant economic force that shaped California's growth. Thousands of Chinese workers were brought to California to help build the railroads, working under near-slavery conditions. The transcontinental railroad network was completed when the two railroads were joined by the famous "gold spike" at Promontory, Utah, in 1869.

But, in the 1890s, things changed for the "octopus," the name given to the railroad companies. William Randolph Hearst, who inherited the San Francisco Examiner newspaper from his father, started an ongoing crusade against the Big Four by publishing critical articles and pointed political cartoons.

# HIGHWAYMAN HUNTINGTON TO THE VOTERS OF CALIFORNIA:

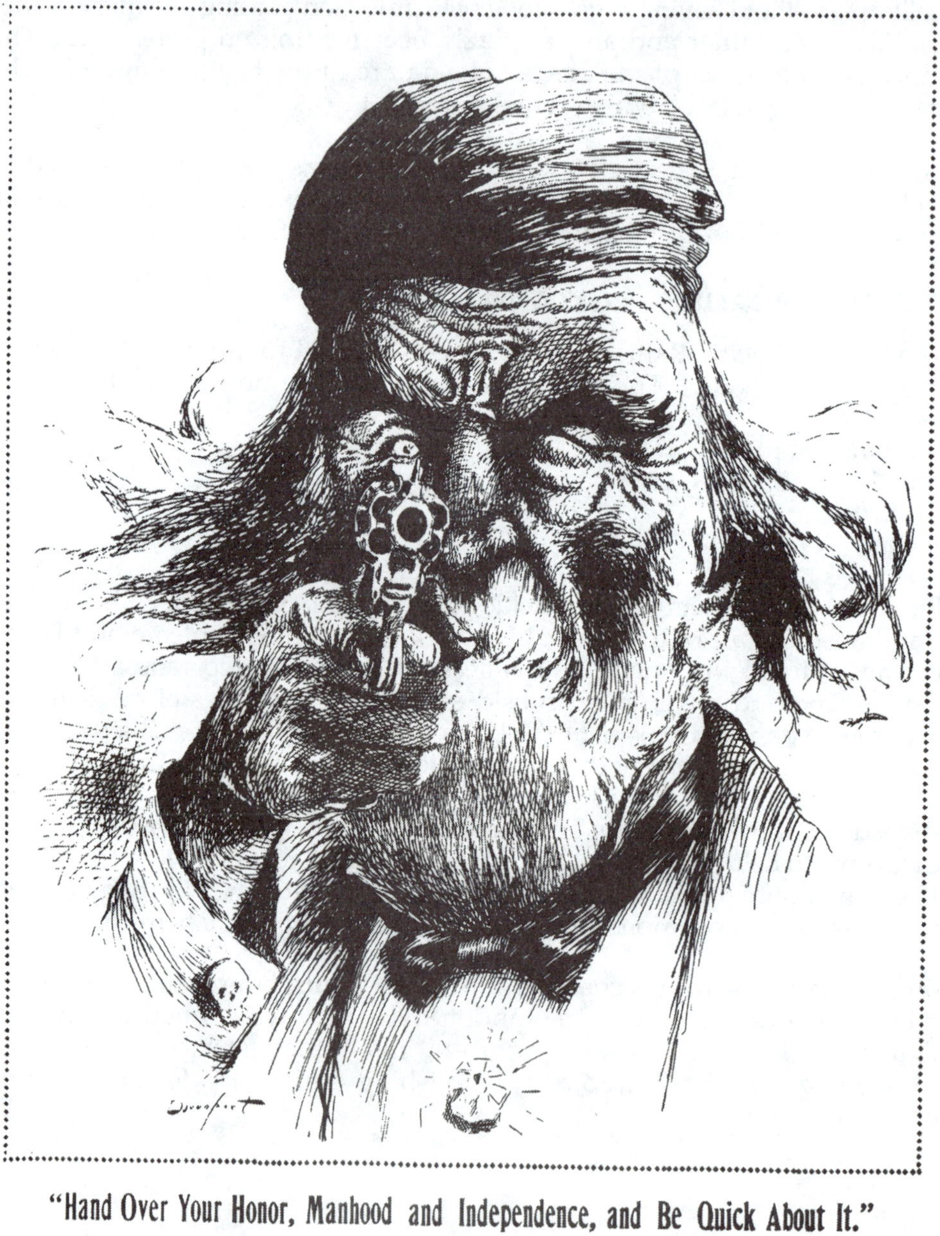

Bancroft Library

"Hand Over Your Honor, Manhood and Independence, and Be Quick About It."

Thanks to the Bancroft Library

# The New Octopus?

***Indian Tribes have a voter-approved gaming monopoly, but will they pay their fair share?***

The California Indian Tribes have a voter-approved monopoly of state slot machine gambling. Casinos built by California tribes receive estimated gaming revenues of $5 billion a year ($500 billion nationally). It is one of the largest and most profitable business (a true monopoly) in the state with no direct competition. Profits are increasing rapidly, and with Governor Schwarzenegger's intent to share in those profits, they will no doubt increase even faster.

The **FEDERAL INDIAN GAMING REGULATORY ACT** *limits Indian tribes' inherent right to have Indian land gambling.* Indian nations, the sole owners and primary gaming beneficiaries, must negotiate with the individual states about the scope of gambling games regulated and played. In 1999, Tribal state gaming compacts were entered into between California and 61 Indian tribal governments, including non-gaming tribe revenue sharing, environmental protections, and labor agreements.

Indian Tribes have since contributed $120 million to both parties' campaigns making some voters wary of Indian tribe political influence. It became a political issue in the 2003 recall election.

Governor Schwarzenegger criticized the Indian Tribes as special interests. He revived Governor Hiram Johnson's memory, whose goal was to "kick the Southern Pacific Railroad out of state politics forever," a railroad compared to an octopus for its grip on state political power.

Governor Schwarzenegger intends to reduce the tribe's political influence and increase the state's casino take. He has called for the Indian casinos to "pay their fair share" (like Connecticut's 25% of tribe's gaming profits) to help shrink the enormous California budget deficit.

California and all California Indian Tribes would both benefit by renegotiating the compacts to:

1. add more slot machines to increase the percentage of California revenues; and
2. add Indian gambling to urban locations.

**The authors do not condone gambling—the average player loses over the long run! You can't beat the house.**

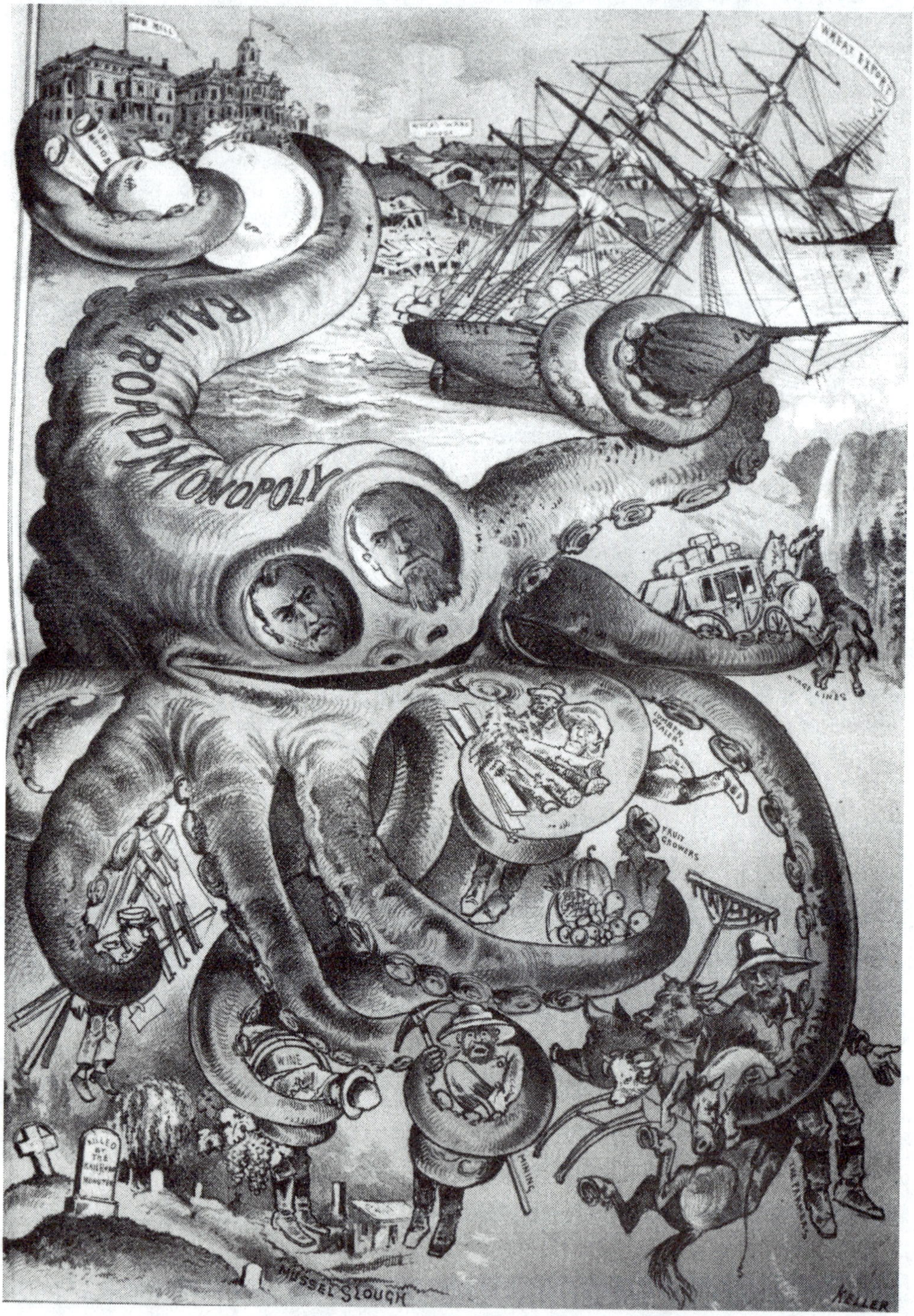
RAILROAD MONOPOLY
LUMBER DEALERS
FRUIT GROWERS
MUSSEL SLOUGH
KELLER

# Early California History and the Federal Government

## CALIFORNIA'S SECOND CONSTITUTION

The **WORKINGMEN'S PARTY** *was an anti-railroad group that disapproved of the large number of unemployed Chinese abandoned in the wake of the railroad construction. Their reform measures, which were later approved by the state legislature, included: a public school system, an eight-hour work day, land monopoly laws, restrictions on Chinese labor, and laws defining the responsibility of corporate directors and officers. The movement was so strong that the **SECOND CALIFORNIA STATE CONSTITUTION** (1879) was adopted and later ratified by the voters after a special constitutional convention.*

*A **CONSTITUTIONAL CONVENTION** is an accepted method to alter a state's constitution or to write an entirely new document, which is submitted to the electorate for a ratification vote.*

## THE CALIFORNIA PROGRESSIVES (REFORMERS)

In the early part of the 20th century, the Southern Pacific Railroad (its new name) was still monopolizing California's politics and manipulating politicians. But the California Progressive Party changed this situation. The **PROGRESSIVES** *were a group of reform-minded Republicans who split from the party to enact permanent changes in the political system that are the basis of the election laws today.*

Hiram Johnson, the new Progressive governor, pushed for political reforms. Among the reform measures passed in 1911 were the: initiative, referendum, recall, direct primary, nonpartisan city and county elections, and a civil service system. The Progressives introduced direct democracy into the California political system. See Chapter 4 for more details.

## *The Federal Government: State vs. Federal Powers*

In this part of the chapter we look at the **two arenas** in which California Politics unfolds. The **first arena** is California's representatives to the federal system: the U.S. Senate and the U.S. House of Representatives. We will also look at the Presidency of the United States. The rest of this chapter is devoted to how this federal system is played out on the California political stage and how the state gets money from the federal government.

The **second arena** is pure California: our governor and our state legislature. Every chapter, except this one, will discuss only California political matters.

**Chapter 2**

# Let's Work Together... for California

**Can Our Congressional Representatives Work Together?**

The **CALIFORNIA CAUCUS** *is all of the U.S. Representatives from California who form a network to coordinate legislation beneficial to our state.* They are supposed to work together so that legislation beneficial to California is passed. However, they seem to be concentrating their voting power more towards party politics rather than our state's interests. What California needs is cooperation. Let's put partisan politics aside and come out with a clear set of objectives to benefit California.

Governor Schwarzenegger has complained that California taxpayers get only 77 cents back in federal funds for every $1 we send to Washington. Who is making sure California is getting its fair share?

## CERTAIN POWERS ARE RESERVED FOR THE STATE

The highest source of power in the United States is the U.S. Constitution, but certain powers are reserved for the states. The 10th Amendment to the Constitution of the United States reads:

> "The powers not delegated to the United States by the Constitution, nor prohibited by it to the States, are reserved to the States respectively, or to the people."

Among other powers reserved solely for the states are the powers to:

1. Establish and control local governments
2. Conduct elections
3. Allow for the formation of business corporations
4. Establish civil and criminal laws
5. Utilize police powers

Of the various powers reserved for the state, police power is probably one of the most important. **POLICE POWER** *permits the state to take action to protect the public health, safety, morals, and welfare of its citizens.*

Some powers are concurrent. **CONCURRENT POWERS** *are powers shared by both the state and the federal government.* Two very important concurrent powers are the ability to tax and to borrow money.

# Early California History and the Federal Government

## Money from Washington

In the last three decades the federal government has been giving money to the states and local governments to help with certain programs. These financial incentives are the federal government's way of influencing and coaxing each individual state to do what Washington, D.C. wants it to do. It is a way to redistribute taxes collected by the federal government to the states. In the 1960s, the federal government began sharing 15% of the nation's budget with the states and local governments, and by 1980, this figure had risen to an all-time high of 23%. The method that the federal government uses to make money available to the states is called grant-in-aid.

### GRANT-IN-AID

*GRANT-IN-AID is money given from one governmental body to another for a specific purpose.* These grants come with strings attached from the U.S. Congress. Most grants require matching funds. *MATCHING FUNDS are federal monies given to the state or local governments that must be matched, dollar for dollar, or they will not be granted.*

Grant-in-aid is disbursed in two different ways: categorical grants and block grants. *CATEGORICAL GRANTS are grants made for a specific purpose or to target a specific program. The restrictions of this type of grant leave the recipient with very little discretion.* Two examples of categorical grants are programs for AIDS patients and the homeless.

The opposite of a categorical grant is a block grant. *A BLOCK GRANT is the awarding of money for general purposes from one level of government to another.* Of the 400 grants-in-aid available, only 14 are currently block grants. This type of grant allows the recipients the freedom to allocate the money among individual programs. For example, if a block grant is for mass transit, it can be used for buses, trains, or construction of stations.

*WELFARE, a state administered program*, was a huge federal program, but now California must decide how best to direct it.

Many of these federal grant-in-aid programs have worked to remove gross inequities among the states. But remember—these programs are highly political. For example, the 1984 Highway Act reduced the amount of money available to states that allowed those under 21 years of age to consume alcoholic beverages. Within four years, every state in the union had a minimum drinking age of 21.

**Chapter 2**

## CALIFORNIA'S PART IN THE U. S. CONGRESS

The *U.S. CONGRESS is made up of two U.S. Senators from California and 53 California members to the U.S. House of Representatives.* California has the largest contingent to the Congress. California's ability to influence national legislation is high, but their ability to organize as a pro-California coalition is another question. The current number of Democratic and Republican representatives is fairly evenly split, making it difficult for them to organize a pro-California coalition.

## FEDERAL AND CALIFORNIA LEGISLATURES

Because of the possible confusion between the legislative houses of the United States and California, a U.S. Senator will always have the "U.S." in front of the word "Senator" and a "state senator" will be referred to as such. Similarly, a member of the U.S. House of Representatives must be distinguished from the state assembly to the California legislature in Sacramento. For a complete breakdown of the State legislature, see Chapter 7.

## U.S. SENATE (U.S. SENATORS)

A *U.S. SENATOR is one of two representatives from each state who altogether form the upper chamber of the federal legislature consisting of 100 members.* California can elect only two members to the U.S. Senate. Each U.S. Senator must be at least 30 years of age and have been a U.S. citizen for nine years. A U.S. Senator serves a six-year term. The two U.S. Senators from California may represent the largest concentration of citizens in the U.S., but each have only two votes.

U.S. Senators are elected from the entire state. A candidate for the U.S. Senate must spend a large amount of time and money campaigning throughout the state.

An *INCUMBENT is the person currently occupying a specific elective office.* Our federal system greatly favors the incumbent U.S. Senate and the current U.S. House of Representatives member, because of their name recognition and an already established campaign organization.

## U.S. HOUSE OF REPRESENTATIVES

*U.S. CONGRESSIONAL MEMBER is the term used to address a member of the U.S. House of Representatives.* There are 53 Congressional members of the House of Representatives elected from California. Although they receive the same salary as a U.S. Senator ($154,700), they do not enjoy the same recognition due to the fact that there are only two of the latter. In 2002, California added one congressional member because our population had

# Early California History and the Federal Government

**CALIFORNIA POPULATION STATISTICS ACCORDING TO U.S. CENSUS**
www.census.gov

| | | | |
|---|---|---|---|
| 1850 - | 92,000 | 1930 - | 5,677,251 |
| 1860 - | 379,994 | 1940 - | 6,907,387 |
| 1870 - | 560,247 | 1950 - | 10,586,223 |
| 1880 - | 864,694 | 1960 - | 15,717,204 |
| 1890 - | 1,213,398 | 1970 - | 20.1 million |
| 1900 - | 1,485,053 | 1980 - | 23.9 million |
| 1910 - | 2,377,549 | 1990 - | 30 million |
| 1920 - | 3,426,861 | 2000 - | 33.9 million |
| | | 2010 - | 39.7 million (projected) |

increased slightly. Since our population is still increasing, the only question is how many new members will we add in 2012.

California's members to the U.S. House of Representatives (all members serve only a two-year term) are generally not known throughout the state because they are elected from districts spread throughout the state.

www.house.gov (House of Representatives)
www.senate.gov (Senate)
www.whitehouse.gov (President)

## State and Federal Reapportionment

### REDISTRICTING MEANS POLITICAL POWER

Redistricting takes place each decade after the U.S. Census is completed. The information gathered from the 2000 census will not be updated until the 2010 census. *REDISTRICTING (reapportionment) is the process by which our state legislature redraws the district lines for California's members of the U.S. House of Representatives, and at the same time, redraws district lines for its own state legislature.*

### REDISTRICTING: POWERFUL LEGISLATIVE TOOL

The political party that controls the state legislature has the "assured power" in California to decide how state legislative districts and federal congressional districts are to be drawn. The legislature is obligated to divide these districts in a way that serves the interests of the citizens living there.

**Chapter 2**

Currently, the Democratic party controls both the California Senate and the California Assembly. Because the Governor has the power to veto the legislature's plan for redistricting, the legislature can only go so far in fixing the voter pattern within each redrawn district or the governor may reject the plan.

## Chapter Summary

The Native Americans, or Indians, were California's first inhabitants. They numbered around 150,000 before the Europeans arrived to "settle" the region. By 1900 there were only around 16,000 Indians left.

The Spanish arrived next. Juan Rodriquez Cabrillo sailed up the west coast and was the first European visitor to California (1542). Father Junipero Serra established a chain of missions starting in 1769. Each mission was a day's horseback ride from the next. Presidios (frontier forts) were established to protect the missions. Pueblos (small settlements) also sprang up at places like San Jose and Los Angeles.

In 1821, Mexico broke from Spain. Huge land grants in California parceled grazing land into ranchos. California broke from Mexico and became a U.S. possession under the Treaty of Guadalupe Hidalgo in 1847. The next year, gold was discovered at Sutter's Mill in the Sacramento area. Gold fever resulted in a massive population growth that has hardly slowed since the time of the "forty-niners." Statehood followed on September 9, 1850, when the state constitution was approved and California joined the union as the 31st state.

Railroads were the dominant force in the new state's economic growth for fifty years. The "Big Four" of the Central Pacific Railroad (Stanford, Huntington, Hopkins, and Crocker) wielded unquestionable political and economic power. The construction of the transcontinental railroad brought thousands of Chinese to California to work under near-slavery conditions. Changes in the California constitution were framed to restrict Chinese labor but they also brought into effect some of the great progressive elements of our state system: free public schools, the eight-hour workday, laws governing monopolies and corporations, and the tools of direct democracy: recall, referendum, and initiative. The Progressive Party under Governor Hiram Johnson furthered this progressive movement with more constitutional reforms in 1911.

# Early California History and the Federal Government

Police powers, the right to protect the public health, safety, morals and welfare, are held by the state while certain concurrent powers, such as taxing and borrowing money, are shared with the federal government. California has two seats in the United States Senate and 53 congressional seats in the United States House of Representatives. We have more representatives in Congress than any other state. And with each new census, we can expect that number to continue to increase.

## Class Discussion Questions

1. What were the contributing factors that lead to the demise of the California Native Americans?

2. What was the "function" of the mission system in California?

3. What political issues did the second California State Constitution in 1879 change?

4. Explain what powers the 10th amendment to the constitution of the United States gives the state of California.

5. What is redistricting, and whom does it protect?

# Chapter 3
# Voters, Primaries, and General Elections

www.ss.ca.gov (Secretary of State)
www.calvoter.org (Nonpartisan)
www.smartvoter.org (League/Women Voters)

## WHO MAY VOTE?

You are eligible to register to vote in California if you meet the following criteria:

1. You are 18 years old or older by election day.
2. You are a U.S. Citizen.
3. You are a resident of California.
4. You are not in prison or on parole for a felony.
5. You haven't been found incompetent by a judge.

Source: *A Guide for Voter Registration in California*, prepared by the the Secretary of State's office in Sacramento.

## REGISTER TO VOTE (WE ALL ENCOURAGE THIS)

In order to vote you must be a registered voter. A **REGISTERED VOTER** is an eligible voter who has filled out an affidavit of registration and delivered it to the county clerk's office or registrar of voters at least 15 days before an election. The Secretary of State oversees the voting process, but the actual administering of the voting is a county and city function.

## FOR YOUR INFORMATION

The registration of a voter is permanent, unless canceled by the registrar of voters. If you move into a new precinct, change your name, or change

### Chapter 3

your political party, you should correct this information with your county registrar of voters as soon as possible. All of the information on your voter registration form is public information that can be obtained by anyone for his or her own personal use.

## MUST A PERSON READ ENGLISH TO VOTE?

NO! Prior to 1970, a Californian had to demonstrate that he or she could read the U.S. Constitution in English before being eligible to register. The Federal Voting Rights Act Amendment, as well as certain California Supreme Court decisions, allows citizens to vote who speak or write only in a language other than English. A person who cannot speak or write at all may also vote.

## *Primary Elections*

In California the primary election is made up of three different elections, all on the same ballot.

The ***PRIMARY ELECTION*** *includes the following: 1) A direct and closed primary that selects partisan (political party) candidates for statewide offices; 2) A nonpartisan primary that selects county and judicial officials, county party officials and the State Superintendent of Public Instruction; and 3) A presidential primary that selects state delegates, from each political party, to their national nominating convention for president and vice president.*

### DIRECT PRIMARY ELECTIONS

A ***DIRECT PRIMARY*** *is an early election for the purpose of selecting partisan candidates from among those nominated by qualified parties.* It places the final responsibility of candidate selection with the voters, not the political party itself. A direct and closed primary eliminates the need for a party convention to select the party's candidates for a given office.

### CALIFORNIA NOW USES A CLOSED PRIMARY

California has its primary election on the first Tuesday after the first Monday in June of even-numbered years. It is a closed primary. In a ***CLOSED PRIMARY***, *a voter can only receive a ballot for the party in which he or she is registered, with the exception of Independents, who may vote in the party primary of their choice.* By contrast, in ***BLANKET PRIMARIES***, *voters can decide who they want for any office position on the ballot no matter what political party the candidate is from.*

## *Voters, Primaries, and General Elections*

## *Closed Primaries... Now in California*

In a blanket primary, everyone receives the same ballot and someone could vote, for example, to nominate a Democratic candidate for governor, a Republican for senator, and a Green Party member for attorney general.

The California Democratic, Republican, Libertarian, and Peace and Freedom parties challenged the state's blanket primary and lost in federal court, and then in the 9th Circuit Court of Appeals.

They claimed the blanket primary affected their ability to chose nominees who represent each party's ideology. The U.S. Supreme Court agreed and voted seven to two to overturn the previous decision.

California now has a closed primary, with the exception of Independents, who are allowed to vote in the party primary of their choice.

## NONPARTISAN OFFICES IN THE PRIMARY

A *NONPARTISAN PRIMARY* is a primary election to nominate a candidate for which no political party may legally nominate a candidate, such as judges, school boards, county and municipal offices, and the State Superintendent of Public Instruction. The election of supreme court judges and appellate court judges is handled differently (see Chapter 8 on Courts). A person who wishes to seek the nomination for a nonpartisan office simply declares his or her candidacy and gathers the signatures required to get on the ballot.

A nonpartisan primary election differs greatly from a partisan primary election in one important aspect: **A nonpartisan primary candidate who receives a majority vote in a primary election wins the office instantly without the need of going on to a general election.** A *MAJORITY VOTE* means that more than fifty percent of the votes cast support one candidate. If no candidate receives a majority vote in the primary, a run-off election between the two individuals with the largest number of votes takes place in the up-coming general election.

# Chapter 3

## THE PRESIDENTIAL PRIMARY

The **PRESIDENTIAL PRIMARY** *is the direct election of delegates to the national party conventions that select nominees for the offices of president and vice president of the United States.* The presidential primary is combined with the regular California primary that is held on the first Tuesday after the first Monday in March of each presidential election year (any year evenly divisible by the number four). The delegates selected go to the national party convention, which is usually held in July or August.

## General Elections

The **GENERAL ELECTION** *is the election held throughout the nation on the first Tuesday after the first Monday of November in even-numbered years.* Court decisions and federal laws have made voter qualifications and election days uniform across the country. More people vote in general elections because of the national media visibility of the candidates.

**The big distinction is that, in a primary election, the nominee wins only the right to run as the party candidate, whereas in the general election he or she does win the office.**

## WHO VOTES IN CALIFORNIA

Exit polls have shown over and over that the largest segment of the population that votes has many things in common. Here is what the typical voters in California have in common:

1. Over 80% are white,
2. Most are homeowners, not renters,
3. Most voters are older, with no children at home, and
4. Most have a post-high school education.

A high percentage of the younger adults and minorities do not register to vote, or vote as regularly as the older, white population. But it is only a matter of time until Asians, Hispanics, and younger people wake up and join the political process. This group of non-voters is like a sleeping giant just waiting for someone to wake it up and make it aware of its political power. Jessie "The Body" Ventura was elected Governor of Minnesota by the usual non-voters who decided to vote.

# Voters, Primaries, and General Elections

## Special Elections

A **SPECIAL ELECTION** *is usually called by the governor to fill unexpired terms and to decide certain ballot measures.* If there is a vacancy in a U.S. congressional or state legislative office, the governor must call for a special election. When a vacancy occurs in a U.S. Senate or U.S. House of Representative's position after the close of the nomination period in the final year of the congressional term, the governor may, at his or her discretion, decline to call a special election and appoint a replacement.

### ELECTIONS ARE CONSOLIDATED

**CONSOLIDATED ELECTIONS** *mean that the elections for different levels of government are put together on the same ballot on the same election date in order to save money and effort.* For example, the presidential primary, on the federal level, is consolidated with the statewide, direct, and nonpartisan primary. This happens only once every four years.

The regularly scheduled election dates for each year are:

#### LOCAL (MUNICIPAL) ELECTION DATES

**April** (2nd Tuesday of even-numbered years) or **March** (1st Tuesday, after the 1st Monday of odd-numbered years)

#### STATEWIDE ELECTION DATES

**June** (1st Tuesday, after the 1st Monday each year)
**November** (1st Tuesday, after the 1st Monday each year)

Elections held in June and November of each even-numbered year are considered California's statewide election dates.

## Precincts and Ballots

### PRECINCTS AND POLLING PLACES

The county registrar of voters divides the county into voting precincts. A **PRECINCT** *is a geographical area made up of a group of voters from a low of 60 to a high of approximately 600, depending on the election and how the registrar of voters wants the voters grouped.*

Each precinct has a precinct board. The board is made up of one inspector, two judges, and three clerks. Each board member must be a voter from that

**Chapter 3**

# CALIFORNIA VOTERS' TIME SCHEDULE

**Registration** – ANY TIME (at least 29 days before election)

**Primaries** – MARCH (first Tuesday after first Monday)

I. Direct Closed Primary (NOMINATING CANDIDATES)

   U.S. SENATORS (2), U.S. HOUSE OF REPRESENTATIVES (53), STATE SENATORS (40), STATE ASSEMBLY MEMBERS (80)

II. Nonpartisan Primary (election at primaries)

   STATE SUPERINTENDENT OF PUBLIC INSTRUCTION, JUDICIAL, AND COUNTY OFFICERS, COUNTY PARTY COMMITTEE MEMBERS

III. Presidential Primary (PRESIDENT)

   NATIONAL PARTY CONVENTION DELEGATES

## General Elections

NOVEMBER (first Tuesday after first Monday in even numbered years)

   PRESIDENTIAL and GUBERNATORIAL ELECTIONS

MARCH/APRIL (second Tuesday in March or second Tuesday in April or at the primary or general elections)

   COUNTY SUPERVISORS, MAYORS, COUNCIL MEMBERS, TREASURERS, CLERKS, AND OTHERS

## Special Elections

ANY TIME UNEXPIRED TERMS: (called by governor or local government)

   U.S. SENATORS, U.S. HOUSE OF REPRESENTATIVES, STATE SENATORS, STATE ASSEMBLY MEMBERS

## Voters, Primaries, and General Elections

### District vs. At-Large Elections

A continuing controversy in California involves the at-large versus the district method of electing local government officials. **AT-LARGE** *is the process of electing local government officials from a group of candidates whose nominations are not based on where they reside, as is the case with district elections.* Only about 5% of the cities and counties in California use the district method.

With at-large elections, the interests of the whole are put ahead of individual neighborhoods. Being elected at-large does not prohibit the election of qualified candidates from the same residential area; the best qualified should be allowed to serve.

District election supporters claim that allowing more than one officeholder per neighborhood is unfair, mainly because the officeholders generally reside in the most affluent areas.

---

precinct or from a precinct in that area. Any voter may apply to be one of these precinct workers, who usually volunteer for the position. You, as students, can gain important political insight from being a precinct volunteer during a long election day. The *POLLING PLACE (POLL) is the location within a precinct where the voting takes place.* Schools and public buildings are popular polling places because these types of structures are available free of charge. A polling place can be just about anywhere, except a bar or liquor store.

### ELECTION DAY

On election day, the polls open at 7am and close at 8pm. This makes for a 13-hour voting period.

### ABSENTEE BALLOT

An *ABSENTEE BALLOT is a ballot that is sent to you before the election, if you choose not to vote in person at the polling place on election day.* It must be received back before the close of the polls. You must apply in writing in order to receive an absentee ballot. Any registered voter may apply for permanent absentee voter status. If you are a permanent absentee voter, you will automatically receive an absentee ballot for each election.

**Chapter 3**

The absentee ballot has become very popular in recent years. In many campaigns part of the campaign strategy is to send absentee ballot request forms to anyone who supports a particular candidate, whether it is requested or not.

## CALIFORNIA DOES NOT PURGE

A *VOTER PURGE is when the registrar of voters goes through the list of registered voters on a systematic basis and eliminates certain voters from the list.* The usual reason is that the voter has not voted in the last general election. In California there is no annual purge of the voter registration roster.

## CALIFORNIA'S BALLOT FORMS

California uses a long ballot form. A *LONG BALLOT is a complete list of the offices, items, and propositions to be decided upon by the voters.* We have eleven state executives to elect other than the governor, as well as judges, county officials, and city officials, plus ballot propositions, bond issues, and maybe a charter amendment or two. We may complain about the length of the ballot, but we are reluctant to give up the privilege of deciding many issues ourselves.

California uses the office-block type of ballot. An *OFFICE-BLOCK BALLOT presents all the competing candidates, by office, throughout the ballot.* The voter makes his or her choice in an office-by-office manner. In contrast, some other states use a *PARTY-COLUMN BALLOT, which lists the candidates party-by-party.* At the top of a party column ballot is a box where a single mark will cast a vote for all of the party candidates. In California, however, it is difficult to vote a party ticket. The office-block ballot forces voters to think of candidates as individuals rather than as part of a partisan ballot ticket.

# Voters, Primaries, and General Elections

## Chapter Summary

Everything in California politics is structured around our two major political parties, Democratic and Republican, although minor political parties play an important role, often bringing new issues and ideas into the mainstream. When you register to vote, you are asked to choose a party, which is a factor in every step of the election process.

In California we use a "direct primary" to select our ballot candidates for major state offices. A direct primary allows the voters to pick their party's candidate from a slate of those nominated by the party. The candidates from each party who win the primary election then go up against each other in the general election. California's primary is a closed primary, meaning a voter only receives a ballot for the party in which he or she is registered. Registered Independents are allowed to vote for the party primary of their choice.

In a presidential primary, the voters do not directly choose their party candidate. Instead, voters elect the delegates to the party convention, and these delegates choose the party candidate. If you want to see a certain candidate represent your party on the presidential ballot, you must vote for a delegate pledged to that candidate in the primary.

A non-partisan primary is held to select candidates for offices that are supposed to be non-party oriented, such as judges, school boards, and the State Superintendent of Instruction.

In such an election, if one of the candidates receives more than half the votes, he or she wins the office immediately. If not, the two leading candidates face a run-off. In the run-off election the person with the most votes wins.

A general election is held every other year in California (on the first Tuesday after the first Monday in November in even-numbered years). In presidential election years, voters select from the party candidates nominated by delegates at the party convention the previous summer. In gubernatorial election years, voters choose from party candidates elected directly in the primary election. Congressional candidates, senators, state representatives, judges, school boards, city councils—all types of elected positions that are available—as well as ballot initiatives, will be included in a consolidated election every two years.

A special election is an election other than the scheduled primary or general elections, called at any time by the governor. These are generally called to fill an office vacancy or to decide an important ballot measure.

**Chapter 3**

The county registrar of voters divides the county into voting precincts. Each precinct has its precinct board (one inspector, two judges, three clerks) and a polling place where the voting takes place. Voters may vote by mail with an absentee ballot, which must be sent in before the polls close. On election day in California the polls open at 7am and close at 8pm.

## Class Discussion Questions

1. How is a closed primary different from a blanket primary?

2. What is the presidential primary?

3. Are there more registered Democrats or Republicans in California?

4. What are the main reasons for voter apathy in California?

5. Discuss the three main types of ballots.

# Voters, Primaries, and General Elections

# Chapter 4
# Direct Democracy

www.scu.edu/law/pubs/Props.htm (State)
www.ss.ca.gov/elections/elections_i.htm (Law)

In 1911, amendments to the state constitution gave us the three basic tools of direct democracy:

1. **THE RECALL**
2. **THE DIRECT INITIATIVE**
3. **THE REFERENDUM**

These three tools removed much of the partisan politics from government and gave California voters the right to help set public policy. Hiram Johnson was the father of California's Direct Democracy.

## The Father of California Direct Democracy

**Governor Hiram Johnson, "The Progressive Reformer," Republican Governor – 1911-1917 (two terms).**

Hiram Johnson, the "Progressive" Republican, was overwhelmingly voted into the governor's office because he, as did a majority of voters, disliked the political power of the railroad monopoly that had been building for decades. His goal was to "kick the Southern Pacific Railroad out of politics." A large number of Progressive Republicans and Democrats joined together to support the progressive idea and cause. A *PROGRESSIVE* is *usually thought of as favoring the restriction of corporate influence in politics and expanding the citizens' participation in politics, while protecting the environment and improving working and living conditions.*

# Chapter 4

Hiram Johnson on the campaign trail

The Progressive reformers saw political parties as the instrument that the Southern Pacific Railroad monopoly had used to dominate the state government for over four decades.

The Progressives' main objective was to weaken the political party system in California, dominated by the Southern Pacific Railroad. These reforms are still with us today.

# Direct Democracy

## HIRAM JOHNSON'S PROGRESSIVE REFORMS THAT CHANGED CALIFORNIA

### 1909 REFORMS

**The direct primary law was enacted.** Candidates for public office must be nominated at a special election called a direct primary, not at a party convention, which had been the practice. This eliminated the "behind closed door" selection of party candidates.

### 1911 REFORMS

**The Railroad Commission**, which regulated the railroads and all the utilities, was increased from three to five members who were now appointed by the governor instead of being elected.

**The direct democracy initiative, referendum, and recall**, became part of the state constitution. Now the voters could actually reverse or make laws themselves, or vote an official out of office.

**Judicial and school board elections became nonpartisan.**

**Women obtained the right to vote.** The U.S. Constitution was not amended to include women's suffrage until 1920.

**Office-Block Ballot was introduced.** Voters vote for each office separately.

### 1913 REFORMS

**City, county, and local special district elections became nonpartisan.**

**The leadership and operation of political parties was defined in detail by law.**

**Cross-filing was permitted by candidates, allowing them to run for the same office or each party in the primary election.** Cross-filing was abolished by Governor Earl Warren.

*Hiram Johnson is called the "Father of California Democracy."*

Chapter 4

# Three Tools of Direct Democracy
(Recall, Referendum, and Initiative)

## THE RECALL

The **RECALL** *is a procedure whereby any California state elected official can be removed from public office, before the completion of his or her term.* Any elected official may be recalled for any reason, but the procedure does take time and effort.

California's two U.S. Senators and fifty-three members of the U.S. House of Representatives are exempt from recall because they hold federal offices, which have different removal procedures.

## THE RECALL PETITION

If you do not like the kind of job a public official is doing, you must circulate a petition and get the required number of voter signatures for a recall vote. The exact number of signatures varies with the type of position the official holds.

> **STATEWIDE OFFICE:** To recall an official who holds a statewide office, the recall petition must contain signatures of registered voters equal to 12% of the votes cast for that position in the last election. The voter signatures must come from at least five counties, and number no less than one percent of the votes cast for the office in that county.
>
> California shocked the world, in October 2003, when Governor Gray Davis became the first California Governor to be removed from office by recall. At the same time, Arnold Schwarzenegger was elected to replace Davis as Governor. (See actual petition on next page.)
>
> **NON-STATEWIDE OFFICE:** The recall petition must contain signatures equal to at least 20 percent of the number of votes cast for that position in the last election.
>
> **LOCAL LEVEL:** On the local level, many recall petitions have obtained the required number of signatures and forced a recall vote. It is difficult, however, to initiate a recall for statewide offices and large districts because of the large number of signatures required. A recall petition does, however, get the public's attention. In the past, there have been unsuccessful statewide recall petition drives against Governor Ronald Reagan, Governor Jerry Brown, and Chief Justice Rose Bird.

# Direct Democracy

## PETITION FOR RECALL

TO THE HONORABLE California Secretary of State.

Pursuant to the California Constitution and California election laws, we the undersigned registered and qualified electors of the State of California, respectfully state that we seek the recall and removal of Gray Davis holding the office of Governor, in California.

We demand an election of a successor to that office. Governor of California.

The following Notice of Intention to Circulate Recall Petition was served on 2/5/2003 to Gray Davis:

NOTICE OF INTENTION TO CIRCULATE RECALL PETITION. TO THE HONORABLE GRAY DAVIS:

Pursuant to Section 11020, California Election Code, the undersigned registered qualified voters of the State of California, hereby give notice that we are the proponents of a recall petition and that we intend to seek your recall and removal from the office of Governor of the State of California, and to demand election of a successor in that office. The grounds for the recall are as follows: Gross mismanagement of California Finances by overspending taxpayers' money, threatening public safety by cutting funds to local governments, failing to account for the exorbitant cost of the energy fiasco, and failing in general to deal with the state's major problems until they get to the crisis stage. California should not have to be known as the state with poor schools, traffic jams, outrageous utility bills, and huge debts....all caused by gross mismanagement.

The printed names, signatures, and business or residence addresses of the proponents are as follows: Edward J Costa; J. Wayne Scherffius; John B. Carney; Stephanie L Brown; Donald M. Nelson Sr.; William A. Stenson, Jr.; John A. Burtscher; Destyn R. Vetter; Loren Oliver Todd; Mark A. Hazen; Thomas H. Wells; Adam M Mrotek; Diane M Schachterle; Mary A. Jensen; Charles T. Jensen; Kenneth J. Payne.

To contact proponents: Ted Costa at People's Advocate: (916)482-6175.

The answer of the officer sought to be recalled is as follows: IF YOU SIGN THIS PETITION, IT MAY LEAD TO A SPECIAL ELECTION THIS SUMMER COSTING US TAXPAYERS AN ADDITIONAL $20-40 MILLION. Last November, almost 8,000,000 Californians went to the polls. They voted to elect Governor Davis to another term. Just days after the Governor's inauguration in January, however, a handful of rightwing politicians are attempting to overturn the voters' decision. They couldn't beat him fair and square, so now they're trying another trick to remove him from office. This effort is being led by the former Chairman of the State Republican Party, who was censured by his own party. We should not waste scarce taxpayers' dollars on sour grapes. The time for partisanship and campaigning is past. It's time for both parties to work together on our State's problems. Moreover, the allegations leveled against the Governor are false. As Governor, Davis has vetoed almost $9 BILLION in spending. California, along with 37 other states, is facing a budget deficit due to the bad national economy. The Bush Administration has announced the federal deficit this year will be the biggest in history, $304 BILLION. In these difficult and dangerous times, LET'S WORK TOGETHER, not be diverted by partisan mischief. /s/ Gray Davis Governor Gray Davis 9911 W. Pico Boulevard, Suite 980 Los Angeles, CA 90035

Each of the undersigned states for himself/herself that he or she is a registered and qualified elector of the County of _____, California.

This column for official use only.

| | | |
|---|---|---|
| 1. Print Name | Residence Address | |
| Signature as Registered | City | Zip |
| 2. Print Name | Residence Address | |
| Signature as Registered | City | Zip |
| 3. Print Name | Residence Address | |
| Signature as Registered | City | Zip |
| 4. Print Name | Residence Address | |
| Signature as Registered | City | Zip |
| 5. Print Name | Residence Address | |
| Signature as Registered | City | Zip |

### DECLARATION OF PERSON CIRCULATING SECTION OF RECALL PETITION
(MUST BE IN CIRCULATOR'S OWN HANDWRITING)

I, _____ declare:
   Print Full Name

1. My residence address is _____, _____, in _____, County,
   Street Address    City

California, and I am a registered voter in _____;
                                              County

2. I personally circulated the attached petition for signing;
3. I witnessed each of the appended signatures being written on the petition and to my best information and belief, each signature is the genuine signature of the person whose name it purports to be; and
4. The appended signatures were obtained between the dates of _____ and _____, inclusive.
                                                                  Starting Date    Ending Date

I declare under penalty of perjury under the laws of the State of California that the forgoing is true and correct.

Executed on _____ at _____, California.
              Date         City or Community Where Signed

SIGNED _____

Chapter 4

## HOW DOES A RECALL WORK?

The recall petition must state the grounds for removal. It can be as simple as a statement that the individual is not doing his or her job. Public officials need not do anything illegal to be recalled.

The recall petition must be filed with the California Secretary of State within a given time period, the maximum being 160 days of being circulated. If the required number of valid signatures has been obtained, the governor must call for a recall election within 180 days after the Secretary of State has certified the accuracy of the petition. The recall ballot is divided into two distinct parts. First, the voters must decide the simple question:

> "Shall _____ be removed from the office of _____ by recall?
> Vote YES or NO."

Also included are the charges against the public official and the incumbent's own statement in defense of these charges.

If the vote is "no" in the recall election, the incumbent remains in office and the recall effort has failed. The incumbent is now protected for at least six months because no new recall petition can be initiated until six months after the last recall election. In addition, the state reimburses the incumbent for all election expenses if the recall election fails.

A majority "yes" vote will remove the public official from office. If this occurs, the voters must then decide who his or her replacement will be. The recall ballot includes a list of candidates from which the voters may choose a replacement for the recalled public official. All that is needed by a candidate to be elected after a recall is a simple majority (plurality) of the votes cast.

Do not confuse recall with impeachment. Recall is initiated by the voters for any reason. **IMPEACHMENT** *is conducted by the state legislature to remove an official from office for a serious violation of the law.*

## LOCAL OFFICIAL RECALLS

Local governments set their own requirements for recall elections under the guidelines handed down by the state legislature. For example, no local government recall may require more petition signatures than a number equal to 25 percent of the votes cast at the last election for that office. The legislature further requires that city recall elections not have a successor

# Direct Democracy

section on a recall ballot. The city council either appoints a new official, or the voters will choose the new official at the next election.

## GOVERNOR RECALLED

Two years of a continuing budget crisis prompted Congressional Representative Darrell Issa to fund a "Petition" to recall Governor Gray Davis. The general public faulted Governor Davis and the Legislature for mismanaging the energy crisis, overspending during the stock market bubble, and the resulting tax increases, including a 300% increase in auto registration fees (taxes).

---

### Drivers' Licenses for Illegal Immigrants!

Former Governor Gray Davis, in a last ditch effort to sway more votes his way before the recall, signed a law allowing illegal aliens to obtain California drivers' licenses. After twice vetoing similar legislation (with more built-in security provisions), Davis had a sudden "change of heart" and signed it into law. He claimed the legislation was intended to make the streets safer, but, because a California driver's license has always been considered proof of identification and legal residency, it may do just the opposite. Without any indication that the licensee is an illegal alien, law enforcement, the FBI, and common sense tell us that, in light of the 9/11 attacks, this law may actually endanger us.

---

The legislature kept passing large spending measures and anti-business regulations during the recall petition period and recall election. When former Governor Davis signed these bills into law, the public perceived him as being out of touch and pandering to special interest voting groups.

Over 134 candidates quailifed for the recall ballot by paying the $3,500 filing fee, obtaining 10,000 signatures, or by a combination of the two. The world's attention turned to California for lively debates and the election.

Arnold Schwarzenegger won, but he still faced an additional $8 to $12 billion deficit the day he took office.

## REFERENDUM (BY PETITION)

*A **REFERENDUM (BY PETITION)** is the process of suspending the implementation of a law passed by the legislature (with the approval of the governor over his or her veto) until it can be voted on by the electorate.*

**Chapter 4**

Do not confuse this with the compulsory referendum. The *COMPULSORY REFERENDUM automatically requires voters at an election to approve a legislature-approved constitutional amendment, charter, or bond issue before it can become law.*

The referendum by petition, which suspends a statute before becoming law, requires the signatures of at least five percent of registered voters who cast votes for governor in the last election. The Secretary of State certifies that the petition has the required number of signatures and is submitted on time (within 90 days after enactment of the bill at a regular session and 91 days after a special session). If the referendum petition qualifies, the law is not enforceable until after the next election, where the voters have a chance to formally accept or reject the new law.

Since the enactment of referendum by petition in California, a vote has been called only thirty-nine times and, of those, only twenty-five laws have been repealed. On the other hand, over 180 initiatives have been placed before the voters for their acceptance. The most important referendum to be placed on the ballot was in June 1982, when the Republican minority disagreed with the Democratic-controlled legislature over the Reapportionment Act of 1980. So, by the 1982 elections, voters had placed three related referendum measures on the June ballot. When all three were approved by the voters, the plan for redistricting (U.S. House Representatives, congressional, and state legislative districts) was rejected.

## DIRECT INITIATIVE

The people of California have another wonderful power; they can make laws without the help of the legislature or the governor through a process known as the direct initiative. A *DIRECT INITIATIVE is a process by which the people draft a proposal or constitutional amendment and acquire enough voter signatures to place the issue on the ballot, where it can be decided by all California voters.* The direct initiative can be on any topic, but must be limited to a "single subject." The governor has no veto power over a direct initiative.

## INITIATIVES ARE POPULAR

The longer 150-day qualification period is the key to why so many initiatives are put before the voters. If a trade group, association, or some other type of interest group has the desire, it can usually put an initiative before the people by hiring professionals to circulate the initiative petitions. Today, one can hire a company just to gather initiative signatures. They usually charge the initiative sponsors from 80 cents to $1.25 for each signature.

# Direct Democracy

## PROPOSITIONS ARE GIVEN NUMBERS

The Secretary of State gives an initiative or a referendum a proposition number when it meets the necessary qualification requirements for the ballot. A *PROPOSITION is a qualified ballot measure that is given a number from one of these three sources: (1) referendum petition—prevents laws from going into effect; (2) compulsory referendums—legislatively-approved constitutional amendments and bond issues, which must always be approved by the voters; and (3) direct initiatives—people-approved petitions that can put any issue on the ballot for voter approval.* To avoid confusion with past and current ballot measures, a law was passed to consecutively number propositions starting with the 2002 general election and running in twenty-year cycles. The next cycle will start in 2022.

## VOTER BALLOT PAMPHLETS

A *VOTER BALLOT PAMPHLET is a booklet sent before the election to each voter explaining propositions and ballot measures.* Different positions and issues on the statewide ballot are presented by the Secretary of State while the city and county clerks help clarify local ballot measures. The Secretary of State states:

> "Many rights and responsibilities go along with citizenship. Voting is one of the most important, as it is the foundation on which our democratic system is built. Read carefully all of the measures and all related information contained in this pamphlet. Referendums, legislative propositions, and citizen-sponsored initiatives are designed specifically to give us, the electorate, the opportunity to influence the laws which regulate us all."

## INITIATIVE REFORM

The rejection by voters of numerous initiatives in general elections has opened the door to possible changes in California's initiative process. The question is: are we really ready to change our initiative system?

California voters may not be as dumb as some professional signature-gathering firms think. Have some self-generating initiative organizations gone too far by cranking out too many new initiative campaigns? Interest groups that saw the initiative process fail to get their legislation passed by the voters are instead looking to lobbying the legislature as an answer.

The biggest complaints refer to the initiative qualification requirements. Grassroots groups with little money to spend can't get their propositions to the voter.

**Chapter 4**

Other critics want more disclosure of the interests and political forces supporting or opposing initiatives. Some want to simplify the ballot so that the average voter can read the initiative once and understand it. Good Luck!

## Chapter Summary

During the "Progressive" era when Hiram Johnson was governor of California (1911-1917), sweeping reforms were made in the state election laws, empowering voters with a more direct form of democracy than was previously enjoyed. The direct primary was created, allowing voters from each party to choose their party candidates for major state offices, rather than relying on the traditional party convention. Certain local, judicial, and school board seats became nonpartisan. Women received the right to vote in California (although the federal government didn't catch up until 1920). The office-block ballot was introduced, requiring voters to vote for each office separately, rather than voting for an entire party slate with a single stroke. But the most important progressive reform of this period was the creation of the recall, referendum, and initiative.

The recall is a procedure by which a state official may be removed from office by a vote of the people. This is not impeachment, where an officeholder is removed for a violation of the law. A recall may be (and in 2003 was) based only on public dissatisfaction. A recall petition is circulated and must be signed by a percentage of the voters (this number varies depending on the office). After a maximum period of 160 days of circulation, if the petition has the proper number of signatures, the governor must call for a recall election. The public is asked to vote "yes" or "no" to the recall and to choose a replacement from a list of candidates. The replacement with the most votes will finish out the term. If the public votes "no" to the recall, the officeholder is safe for at least six months, then a new recall can be initiated. In local elections there is no successor section on the recall ballot. The successor is either appointed by the city council or the office remains vacant until the next election.

The recall election on October 7, 2003 stunned the nation and put Arnold Schwarzenegger in the governor's office.

A referendum allows the public to block an unwanted law from taking effect. A petition (signed by at least five percent of the registered voters who cast votes for governor in the previous election) must be presented to the Secretary of State within 90 days of the enactment of the bill, making it unenforceable until after the next election, where the voters may formally reject or accept it.

## Direct Democracy

The direct initiative process allows voters to enact laws for themselves. An initiative is a proposed law or state constitutional amendment initiated by the people. A petition with the proper number of signatures will place an initiative on the ballot for the people to decide in the next election. Initiatives and referendums appear on the ballot as Propositions with a number assigned to each by the Secretary of State.

Remember, only California state and local officials can be recalled. Federal officials cannot be recalled.

## Class Discussion Questions

1. Why is Hiram Johnson referred to as the father of direct democracy in California?

2. What group benefits the most from the recall, the initiative, and the referendum?

3. Can you think of an instance when the recall may be a bad idea and not in the best interest of democracy?

4. Have the people in California come to rely too heavily on the initiative process?

5. Why do you think there is a 150-day limit to gather signatures for an initiative or referendum?

# Chapter 5
# Interest Groups, Political Parties, and Campaigns

## Interest Groups

We have a large state that is very diverse. It is an amazing society of varying interests and ideas. But all interest groups have one thing in common: they want California's elected officials to know how they feel about their pet issues. It is the stated purpose of interest groups to influence people in such a way that interest groups' points of view will be accepted.

An **INTEREST GROUP** *is an organized group having a common interest that attempts to persuade others to see its point of view*. Its objective is to have public policy makers embrace its goals and ideas. For example, the California Association of Realtors® is made up of over 120,000 real estate brokers and salespeople who foster the concept of home ownership, and work to protect their sale's commissions.

Small groups can have much more of a political impact on legislation if they join forces. The League of California Cities, for example, maintains offices, libraries, researchers, and several lobbyists at a fraction of what the cost would be if each city tried to represent its own interest. Almost every city in the state is a member.

### DIFFERENT TYPES OF INTEREST GROUPS

Interest groups differ greatly as to money, size, and goals. **PRIVATE AGENDAS** *are specific objectives set by, in this case, an interest group in order to help it accomplish a specific goal*. These groups are as diverse as the California Trial Lawyers Association and the Sierra Club.

## Chapter 5

### BUSINESS GROUPS

Most large corporations and trade associations have representatives in Sacramento. Apple Computer, Chevron, and other California-based firms protect their interests by having lobbyists in the state capital. *TRADE ASSOCIATIONS are organizations made up of similar businesses whose goal is the promotion of their common interests.* Their goal is straightforward; they want to stay in business by continuing to provide goods or services to the consumer, and, at the same time, make a profit. The California Chamber of Commerce represents many different types of firms, but other trade associations represent specific types of businesses, like the California Manufacturer's Association or the California Retailer's Association.

### DEMOGRAPHIC INTEREST GROUPS

Gays and lesbians are good examples of demographic interest groups, although many of their members may not think of themselves as such. *DEMOGRAPHIC INTEREST GROUPS are groups of people who share characteristics such as income, age, and education.* Although gays and lesbians have made great strides for equality in recent years, as a group they have not fully attained their desired objectives. In the area of AIDS treatment and research, they have done a fine job of educating the general public to the fact that it is a disease of the general population, not just the homosexual population.

### SINGLE-ISSUE GROUPS

Groups formed to publicize only one particular issue or subject are known as *SINGLE-ISSUE INTEREST GROUPS. The Pro-Choice Movement and Right-to-Life Advocates are two such groups.*

### LOBBYISTS

Interest groups hire men and women to represent them in our state capital, Sacramento. These people are referred to as lobbyists.

A *LOBBYIST is a person, acting for specific interest groups, who tries to influence the introduction of legislation and the votes taken on bills in the legislature.* Sometimes lobbyists are referred to as the "third house of the legislature" because they have as much influence over legislation as the Assembly and the Senate.

### WHAT MAKES A SUCCESSFUL LOBBYIST?

Some people may be surprised to find that money, gifts, and expensive meals are not the tools used by a successful lobbyist. Lobbyists are not

# Interest Groups, Political Parties, and Campaigns

## UNIONS, CORPORATIONS, AND PROFESSIONAL ASSOCIATIONS

**1. BUSINESS**
California Chamber of Commerce, California Manufacturers Association, California Bankers Association, California Retailers Association, California Association of Realtors

**2. AGRICULTURE**
California Farm Bureau Federation, Agricultural Council of California, United Farm Workers

**3. LABOR (UNIONS)**
California State Employees Association, California Teamsters Public Affairs Council, California Labor Federation

**4. PROFESSIONAL ASSOCIATIONS**
California Medical Association, State Bar of California

**5. EDUCATION**
Association of California School Administrators, California School Boards Association, California Teachers Association, California Federation of Teachers

**6. GOVERNMENT**
County Supervisors Association, League of California Cities

**7. IDEOLOGICAL ORGANIZATIONS**
American Civil Liberties Union (ACLU)

**8. RACIAL, ETHNIC, OR RELIGIOUS ORGANIZATIONS**
National Association for the Advancement of Colored People (NAACP), Mexican-American Political Association (MAPA), California Catholic Conference

**9. PUBLIC UTILITIES**
Pacific Gas & Electric Company, Verizon

**10. MISCELLANEOUS**
League of Women Voters, California Taxpayers Association, Sierra Club, Girl Scouts, Boy Scouts

**Chapter 5**

usually loud, but are pleasant and non-offensive. A good lobbyist uses "the soft sell approach" by convincing the official that it is important for him or her to listen. A smart lobbyist is well organized, direct, and succinct in his or her presentation. The golden rule is never make a legislator look bad or uninformed.

In Sacramento, where most law-making is done by committee, it is best for the lobbyist to schedule, with the legislator's office, a one or two minute walking meeting between committee meetings.

This lobbying technique is best described by the term "schmooze." *SCHMOOZE is the term used by lobbyists to describe the art of discussing business in a casual, social manner.*

### CROWD LOBBYING

***CROWD LOBBYING** is the practice of mobilizing large numbers of people to attend organized rallies timed to influence a decision or specific legislation.* The group, if successful, will draw news media attention and attain free publicity for its cause.

## Political Parties

### CALIFORNIA'S POLITICAL PARTIES

A ***POLITICAL PARTY** is a large organization of voters who have similar views and band together to gain more power.* Because of our primary elections and the large number of nonpartisan local government positions, the California political party machinery is not as strong as it is in other states.

A recognized political party is entitled to place its candidates' names on the primary ballot. If a political party registers a number equal to at least one percent of the total votes cast in the last gubernatorial election (approximately 80,000), that party will be recognized by the Secretary of State.

The political parties recognized in California are:

| | |
|---|---|
| American Independent | www.woropr.com |
| Democratic | www.ca-dem.org |
| Green | www.rahul.net/greens |
| Peace and Freedom | www.peaceandfreedom.org |
| Natural Law | www.natural-law.org |
| Reform | www.california.reformparty.org |

# Interest Groups, Political Parties, and Campaigns

 www.smartvoter.com

## *League of Women Voters*

The **LEAGUE OF WOMEN VOTERS** *is a nonprofit, nonpartisan volunteer group that educates voters in the areas of issues and public problems.* The League is especially helpful in analyzing complicated ballot measures so that the public can understand the real issues behind a proposition. It is one of the few interest groups that presents its analysis to the general public. This group is also to be applauded for sponsoring debates between candidates in the interest of voter education. Its main goal is to inform the voter. The state organization is listed below, but there are local chapters throughout California.

**League of Women Voters of California**
926 J Street, #1000
Sacramento, CA 95814

| | |
|---|---|
| Republican | www.cagop.org |
| Libertarian | www.ca.lp.org |

After initial recognition by the secretary of state, an organization must maintain a membership equal to at least two percent of the total votes cast in the last gubernatorial election or lose its legal existence.

## DEMOCRATS AND REPUBLICANS

Of course, the two major political parties are the Republicans (GOP) and the Democrats (Dems). Most voters in California are either Democrats or Republicans, but it is very common to cross party lines in the privacy of the voting booth. *TICKET-SPLITTING is when a person votes for different political parties, depending on the office.* For example, people may vote for a Republican governor, a Democratic lieutenant governor, a Republican attorney general and a Democratic state treasurer.

## POLITICAL LABELS

A ***CONSERVATIVE*** *is a person or philosophy that tends to favor established traditions, smaller government, and resistance to change.* We often speak of conservatives as being to the "right" and liberals as the "left." In

**Chapter 5**

American politics, conservatives tend to identify with the Republican party, but a person may also be thought of as a conservative Democrat if he or she identifies with the "right" on certain issues.

A *LIBERAL is a person or philosophy that tends to favor political reform or progress and is open to ideas that challenge established traditions.* Liberals generally lean towards more government spending paid for by increased taxation. In American politics, liberals tend to identify with the Democratic party; however, a person might see himself as a liberal or "moderate" Republican.

Labels such as "conservative" and "liberal" are useful in providing a general idea of where a person stands on certain issues. In reality, however, many or most individuals will fluctuate greatly between these positions, depending on the issue.

## STATE CENTRAL COMMITTEE

Each recognized political party has a State Central Committee and a County Central Committee. The *STATE CENTRAL COMMITTEE is made up of partisan office holders, nominees, appointees, and other minor party officials.* It does not represent the rank-and-file party member.

Each party has large state central committees that are broken down into several parts. The *EXECUTIVE COMMITTEE of each party is a small group of high party officials who meet often to conduct party business in the party name.*

The state central committees adopt resolutions, coordinate fund raising, and encourage party enthusiasm. Campaigning is done by each individual candidate's organization and any helpful interest groups. The State Central Committee's effectiveness is minimal because of California's political traditions and our state's large size.

## COUNTY CENTRAL COMMITTEE

A *COUNTY CENTRAL COMMITTEE is the county political party group elected by popular vote from assembly districts.* Additional members are party nominees from within the district. The Los Angeles area, which forms one of the largest groups, has over three hundred members on the county committee. County party committees have the job of helping candidates with their campaigns, but like the state committees, they have little effect. Besides, a recent statute has prohibited California political parties from endorsing a candidate before the primary election. Our state laws discourage political parties from having a strong and effective state and county representation.

# Interest Groups, Political Parties, and Campaigns

## Smoke-Free Workplace Law

*www.californialung.org*

The Smoke-Free Workplace Law prohibits any smoking in the workplace, including restaurants, offices, factories, and bars. It is designed to protect all employees from exposure to the health risks associated with secondhand smoke in indoor workplaces.

Nearly all California adults employed indoors are now protected as a result of the smoke-free bar provision. Meanwhile, smoke-related diseases go on killing up to 500,000 people each year. For this reason, legislators seem to have no hesitation in continually increasing taxes on tobacco products. These so-called "sin taxes" include alcohol as well as tobacco products. Lawmakers defend raising these taxes so often by claiming they discourage harmful behavior by younger Californians.

## POLITICAL REFORM ACT (PROPOSITION 9)

The ***POLITICAL REFORM ACT** was instituted to oversee more than 100,000 candidates for state and local government, their campaign funds, and the activities of lobbyists.* This proposition ensures that state ballot pamphlets will be an independent, useful document sent to each voter, and that laws or practices unfairly favoring incumbents will be abolished. To achieve these goals, the political reform act provides the following:

1. Conflict of interest rules for government officials.
2. Disclosure requirements for candidates, committees, lobbyists, and public officials.
3. Nonpartisan ballot pamphlets that analyze and present the actual text of existing laws and proposed changes.

***THE FAIR POLITICAL PRACTICES COMMISSION** is a five-member, bipartisan state panel responsible for the administration and enforcement of the Political Reform Act.* The commission may impose direct fines of $2,000, and higher fines through civil suits. All fines are paid into the state treasury, not the agency itself.

## ELECTION LAWS

Several election laws have established that:

1. Legislators cannot receive any gift over $250.

### Chapter 5

## Endorsements and PACs (Political Action Committees)

An **ENDORSEMENT** *is an official show of support to a candidate from an important source.* Endorsements come from interest groups, celebrities, newspapers, other political leaders, and state or county political committees. Endorsements for nonpartisan races were prohibited in 1986 by a constitutional amendment.

In a campaign, real political muscle comes from the ability of a candidate to obtain crucial endorsements and generate campaign contributions, especially from PACs. **PACs (Political Action Committees)** *are subgroups within large organizations, such as corporations, trade groups, unions, and grass roots groups that contribute campaign funds to candidates who support their political view.* It is much easier for a candidate to build a campaign "war chest" from PACs because large contributions are granted with little effort, and they may often include a powerful endorsement.

2. Members of state boards and commissions are now subject to the maximum $250 honorarium and limit on gifts.
3. Legislators are now, for the first time, prohibited from voting on legislation that would be a conflict of interest.
4. Legislators and members of state boards and commissions are prohibited from lobbying the legislature for at least one year after leaving office.

## *Campaigns*

### POLITICAL CAMPAIGNS

Strategy is the key to every well-run political campaign. A *CAMPAIGN STRATEGY is a well-thought-out tactical plan with winning an election as its goal.* This is accomplished by identifying the audience, the message, the delivery, and timing, while considering the campaign resources.

The most important element of a good campaign strategy is to develop a good campaign message. The *CAMPAIGN MESSAGE is the theme of the person or the issue that the campaign will attempt to communicate to voters.* The complex issues of a campaign must be reduced down to a simple message that sets the candidate apart from all others.

# Interest Groups, Political Parties, and Campaigns

## PAST ELECTIONS OFFER VOTER PATTERNS

*VOTER TARGETING is the deliberate attempt on the part of a campaign to identify the precincts or election districts in which to consolidate its effort in order to win.* Voter targeting uses past voter patterns and turnouts as the best indicator of future voting patterns for the same precinct. Precincts that have not been committed to a particular political party are called swing voters.

The *SWING VOTERS are the individual voters who have not committed themselves to a particular political party, issue, or candidate but, if presented with an appealing campaign message, may vote for that issue or candidate.* These swing voters should be the most targeted because this group may produce the biggest switch to your side with the least campaign cost and effort.

A *VOTER LIST is the list of registered voters by name, address, party affiliation and, in California, phone number that is supplied for a small charge, precinct by precinct, to the purchaser from the county registrar of voters.* Not only can individuals or campaigns buy voter lists, but they can also buy precinct results of past elections with a list that identifies who voted in that particular election. But relax—they can not tell anyone how a person actually voted!

## *Campaign Laws in California*

### CALIFORNIA POLITICAL REFORM ACT

All California candidates and political committees must file a periodic campaign statement listing information regarding financial contributions and expenditures. It is filed with the Fair Political Practices Commission in Sacramento. The report must be signed by the filer, under penalty of perjury, confirming that it is true and correct. All advertising must identify the sponsor, and no anonymous contributions over $100 are allowed.

### LOCAL CAMPAIGN ORDINANCES (LAWS)

Local government can adopt its own campaign laws, in addition to the state laws. Some cities and counties have limited corporate contribution amounts and require additional campaign statements.

### FEDERAL ELECTION CAMPAIGN ACT

The Federal Election Campaign Act applies only to people running for federal office. This law requires candidates to file periodic public reports disclosing financial facts about campaign contributions and expenditures.

# Chapter 5

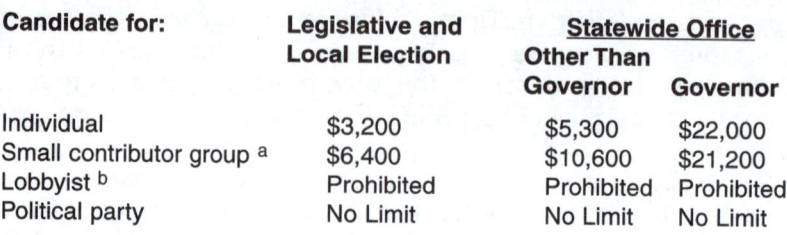

## Proposition 34 Limitations on Contributions

| Candidate for: | Legislative and Local Election | Statewide Office Other Than Governor | Governor |
|---|---|---|---|
| Individual | $3,200 | $5,300 | $22,000 |
| Small contributor group a | $6,400 | $10,600 | $21,200 |
| Lobbyist b | Prohibited | Prohibited | Prohibited |
| Political party | No Limit | No Limit | No Limit |

| Voluntary Limits | Primary | General |
|---|---|---|
| State Assembly | $425,000 | $744,000 |
| State Senate | $637,000 | $956,000 |
| State Board of Equalization | $1.1 Million | $1.6 Million |
| Statewide office, except Governor | $4.2 Million | $6.3 Million |
| Governor | $6.3 Million | $10.6 Million |

a Defined as a committee in existence for at least six months with 100 or more members, none of whom contribute more than $200 to the committee in a year, and which contributes to five or more candidates.

b Prohibition applies to lobbyists only in certain circumstances.

The law also sets limits on the amount of money that can be contributed by individuals at $1,000 and may go as high as $5,000 for groups. Copies of these reports can be examined at the office of the Federal Election Commission in Washington, D.C.

## Casino Gambling In California

Since gambling was legalized, Californian's Indian Tribes have become one of our state's most powerful Special Interest Groups. The Indian Tribes are making billions of dollars without paying state taxes on profits. They have a virtual monopoly on gambling.

Before the recall election, the gubernatorial candidates were falling all over themselves to support reduced regulations on gambling. Ex-Governor Davis even went so far as to offer to put two Indian members on the Gambling Control Commission. Some public policy experts say such

## Interest Groups, Political Parties, and Campaigns

a move would create a perception of corruption if special interest groups gain access based upon campaign contributions. To those experts, its the political equivalent of assigning the "wolf to guard the hen house." Remember; Nevada residents pay no state income taxes because taxing the huge gambling industry pays for almost everything. That state, however, will not let anyone with gambling interests be on the gambling commission. New Jersey, in an attempt to keep the gambling industry free of organized crime, barred casinos from making political contributions.

Since California has welcomed Indian Tribe gaming, it is only prudent to have strict independent regulators that oversee honest casinos and tax them for the benefit of our state. Perhaps we should look to Nevada's strict regulatory scheme as a good model to follow.

Indian Tribes spent over $120 million on state political campaigns in the last five years, which was more than any other industry in the state. Gaming is a very profitable industry, so you can see why the Indians want to minimize taxation and reduce regulation.

### Tribes Recall Donors

Five indian tribes gave more than $6,000,000 directly to candidates and to their campaigns as part of the recall election:

| | |
|---|---|
| Pechanga | $2,538,200 |
| Viejas | $2,017,848 |
| Sycuan | $979,900 |
| Morongo | $553,729 |
| Santa Rosa | $501,000 |

Contributions were targeted to the following recall candidates:

| | |
|---|---|
| Bustamente | $5,149,500 |
| Davis | $396,200 |
| McClintock | $580,000 |
| Schwarzenegger | $0 |

**Californian's Indian Tribes are at the middle of the big debate over the role of campaign contributions in shaping public policy.**

### Chapter 5

## Chapter Summary

Interest groups consist of people with common goals who organize together in an effort to influence public policy making. These groups come in all sizes and types, organized around many different issues: political, economic, cultural, and social. Small, local groups will often band together on a statewide basis to wield more clout.

Interest groups often engage professional lobbyists to represent them. Lobbyists are a big part of the political process in Sacramento, building relationships with lawmakers and persuading lawmakers to support legislation favorable to the groups they represent.

Most politicians align themselves with either of the two major political parties, Democrats or Republicans. Along with the American Independent, Green, and Peace and Freedom, Natural Law, Reform, and Libertarian Parties, these are the eight official parties currently recognized on the state ballot. The Republican Party is generally viewed as more conservative than the Democrats, tending to resist radical change in favor of more established traditions and values. The Democratic Party is perceived as being more liberal, favoring reform and being more open to new ideas. Each party has its own internal structure including a Central Committee, made up of officeholders and party officials throughout the state, and an Executive Committee of highly placed party officials who decide policy. Political parties in California don't actually run a candidate's campaign, but they do play a major advisory and organizational role.

A great effort is made to keep elections fair. The Political Reform Act (Proposition 9) places controls on candidates, lobbyists, and campaign funds. This law is enforced by the bipartisan Fair Political Practices Commission.

Successful political campaigns are based on careful planning and a sound campaign strategy. The campaign message must often be very simple and straight-forward, in order to capture the imagination of the voting public. Voter targeting involves identifying key election districts that should be emphasized in campaigning. Swing voters are those who might be persuaded either way on an issue, depending on the appeal of the campaign message.

Californian's Indian Tribes have become one of our state's most powerful Special Interest Groups since gambling has been legalized.

**Interest Groups, Political Parties, and Campaigns**

## Class Discussion Questions

1. Is it true that only large business corporations form interest groups?

2. Is it true that interest groups only pull America apart and offer the citizens nothing?

3. Do trade associations only protect the weak?

4. Is it true that the third parties will soon take on the Democrats and the Republicans?

5. Is it true that California has no campaign laws?

Chapter 5

# Chapter 6
# The Executive Branch

## Executive Branch

Arnold Schwarzenegger, the current *GOVERNOR OF CALIFORNIA, is the chief executive officer of our state government, and because of California's prominence, he is also an influential figure in national politics.* The governor, however, does not act alone. California uses a plural executive system. The California *PLURAL EXECUTIVE system is one that consists of the governor and eleven other elected officials* (See next page). Each of the other eleven members of the plural executive runs a separate part of the state government. This is different from the federal government, where more power is concentrated in the hands of a single chief executive. The voters decide who holds these positions and quite often they are from a different political party than the governor's. All California plural executives:

1. serve four-year terms;
2. terms start 1st Monday after January 1;
3. have a two-term limit;
4. are subject to recall and impeachment; and
5. vacancies are filled by the governor.

The balance of the governor's administration is made up mostly of political appointees. These appointees include the governor's cabinet, staff, a large, diverse number of directors and commissioners of agencies, departments, and various boards and commissions. The way our state constitution is written, the governor is responsible and accountable to the people for the performance of every member of the administration.

The *ORDER OF SUCCESSION is the descending order of who assumes the governor's office in the event of death, resignation, removal, or disability.* The order of succession for the governor of California is:

# Chapter 6

## California's Plural Executive Officials

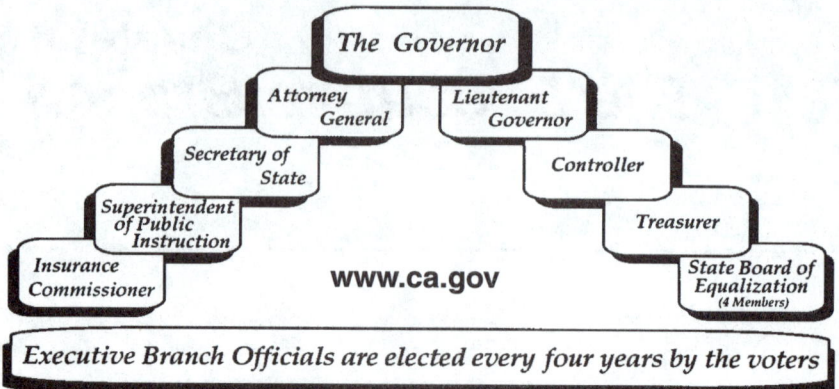

1. Lieutenant Governor
2. President Pro Tempore of the Senate
3. Speaker of the Assembly
4. Secretary of State
5. Attorney General
6. Treasurer
7. Controller

If there is a question about the governor's competence, an appointed commission petitions the State Supreme Court for its determination.

## The Office of Governor

Candidates for governor must meet these state requirements:

1. Citizen of the United States.
2. Qualified to vote.
3. California resident for at least 5 years immediately preceding the election.

### GUBERNATORIAL POWERS

*GUBERNATORIAL* refers to anything having to do with the governor. The gubernatorial powers are those held by the chief executive of the state. They include the following:

78

# The Executive Branch

1. Ceremonial and Political Leader
2. Appointment Power
3. Judicial Influence
4. Commander-in-Chief of the State Militia
5. Legislative Leader

## CEREMONIAL AND POLITICAL PARTY LEADER

The governor is the world representative of California and its citizens. Ceremonial duties include ribbon-cutting, greeting world leaders, and other celebrations.

In addition to running the executive branch, the governor is also the leader of his or her political party, lending strength and prestige to that party. Also, the governor can exercise influence by making appointments, nominations, and shaping the direction of state and local party organizations.

The governor can greatly affect higher education because he or she is automatically the president of both the University of California Board of Regents and the California State University Board of Trustees.

## APPOINTMENT POWER

The governor has appointment power over departments and key policy makers. Several hundred of these appointments are for important board members and commissioners.

When a vacancy occurs due to death, removal, or resignation, the governor also makes appointments to fill the unexpired terms of the following offices:

1. Statewide officers
2. U.S. Senators
3. U.S. House of Representatives
4. County Supervisors
5. Judicial vacancies on the Superior Courts
6. State Supreme Court and Court of Appeal Justices

## JUDICIAL INFLUENCE

The governor has judicial influence through his or her power to nominate judges to the State Supreme Court, the Court of Appeal, and fill vacancies by appointment as they arise. With regard to convicted felons, the governor has the power to pardon, commute sentences, and grant reprieves, but the reason

**Chapter 6**

for granting clemency must be reported to the legislature. *CLEMENCY is the governor's power to reduce or eliminate the sentences of convicted felons for humanitarian reasons.*

The governor may grant a *PARDON, which is the release of the convicted criminal from the legal consequences of the crime.* A governor may commute the sentence. *COMMUTE means a reduction in the length of a prison term.* A *REPRIEVE allows the governor to postpone a sentence of the court from being carried out.*

Without a doubt, the most controversial clemency power is the right of the governor to affect capital offenses. A *CAPITAL PUNISHMENT offense is one where the death penalty is prescribed by the court for the crime of taking, or involvement in the taking of, a human life.*

## COMMANDER-IN-CHIEF OF THE STATE MILITIA

The *COMMANDER-IN-CHIEF is the top official who directs the state militia (national guard).* The governor can call the guard to active duty on his or her own initiative or upon the request of local officials in the event of a civil disturbance or natural disaster.

## LEGISLATIVE LEADER

The legislative leadership is probably the most important power the governor possesses.

The governor is the *LEGISLATIVE LEADER of California because he or she presents a personal agenda and annual budget to the legislature and can exercise this leadership role with veto powers over legislation.*

The *STATE OF THE STATE ADDRESS is a speech by the governor at the beginning of each legislative session in January to inform the state senate and state assembly about the condition of the state, his or her legislative agenda, and recommendations for the year.* An annual state budget covering projected revenues and expenditures is prepared and submitted to the legislature. After the legislature passes its version of the budget back to the governor, the governor may reduce or eliminate particular budget items by use of the line item veto.

A revised budget bill is seldom signed "as is" by the governor. The *LINE ITEM VETO allows the governor to eliminate specific items and amounts from the proposed budget that are not to the governor's liking.* The biggest legislative weapon the governor holds is the full veto. A *VETO is the total rejection of any*

# The Executive Branch

bill that can then only be overridden by a two-thirds vote of both the state assembly and the state senate, as opposed to a simple majority (51%). As a practical matter, a gubernatorial veto is difficult to override.

The constitutional revision of 1966 (extending time for legislative sessions) and the legislative re-organization of 1972 (continuous two-year session) effectively eliminated the pocket veto. A *POCKET VETO* means that a governor fails to take any action on pending legislation after the legislature has adjourned.

## THE POWER TO MAKE LAWS

Bills that have been approved by both houses of the legislature are sent to the governor for his or her signature. The governor has 12 days after receiving the bill to do one of the following:

1. Sign the bill thereby making it a law.
2. Not sign the bill thereby making it law.
3. Veto the bill.

**Remember:** if two-thirds of both houses override the governor's veto, the bill becomes law.

## Administration of the Executive Branch

There are many levels to the executive branch, making it resemble a giant corporation. There are thousands of people and many levels of management.

## THE EXECUTIVE BRANCH APPOINTMENTS:

GOVERNOR'S CABINET
AGENCIES
DEPARTMENTS
DIVISIONS
GOVERNOR'S PERSONAL STAFF *
   (* The staff does not have to be confirmed by the Senate)

## THE GOVERNOR'S CABINET

The *GOVERNOR'S CABINET* is an advisory group that provides the chief executive with a comprehensive overview of state operations and has a hand in policy making and long-term planning for California. Cabinet members must be confirmed by the state senate.

## Chapter 6

## AGENCIES, DEPARTMENTS, AND DIVISIONS

The administrators of these agencies are referred to as "secretaries of the agencies." The secretaries of the agencies provide leadership to the departments so that the governor can communicate efficiently between the numerous departments. The members of the governor's cabinet are usually secretaries of the agencies.

## GOVERNOR'S PERSONAL STAFF

The *PERSONAL STAFF OF THE GOVERNOR is a group of approximately 100 coordinators who assist the governor in a variety of activities with the press, media, legislators, budget analysts, and others.* Usually they were the governor's closest advisors when he or she was a private citizen. Unlike the governor's cabinet, the personal staff is not confirmed by the state senate.

## California's Plural Executive

There are seven state elected officers, other than the governor and the four board of equalization members.

### LIEUTENANT GOVERNOR        www.ltg.ca.gov

The *LIEUTENANT GOVERNOR is elected independently from the governor and, despite his or her title, has very few significant duties to perform in California.* The only official job of the lieutenant governor is to break a tie in the state senate, if such an event happens. The lieutenant governor is also an ex officio member of: the Board of Regents of the University of California, the Board of Trustees of the State University System, and the state lands commission, but these memberships take very little time. The lieutenant governor is given all the powers of governor (state constitution) when the governor is incapacitated, out of the state, or, if there is a vacancy, he or she becomes governor.

### ATTORNEY GENERAL        www.caag.state.ca.us

The *ATTORNEY GENERAL is director of the justice department in California and, as such, he or she is responsible for ensuring that the laws of the state are fairly enforced.* The attorney general is the most important executive officer in the state after the governor, acting as legal counsel for the state and most state agencies. The attorney general is responsible for the preparation of all ballot propositions submitted to the voters in state elections. Quite often the attorney general is from the party opposite that of the governor. The office is often a stepping-stone to governorship, for example: Earl Warren (1942); Edmund "Pat" Brown (1958); and George Deukmejian (1982).

# The Executive Branch

## STATE CONTROLLER

www.sco.ca.gov

The *STATE CONTROLLER is chief accountant for the state*. The controller accounts for, and pays out, all state money. He or she advises local governments on financial matters and, in annual reports to the public, divulges their financial conditions.

The controller chairs the Franchise Tax Board, which is responsible for collection of state income taxes, and sits on the Board of Equalization, which collects the all-important state sales tax. He or she also chairs the State Lands Commission, and sits on the Water Resources Control Board. As you can see, the office of controller in the state of California is a very powerful one.

## TREASURER

www.treasurer.ca.gov

The *TREASURER is responsible for investing in bonds to fund large capital projects, such as construction of highways, schools, and dams*. The Treasurer has the responsibility of auctioning state bonds, having custody of the state money, and shifting state funds into banks and savings institutions that offer the highest interest rates. He or she must pool the various state accounts into a single high-yield investment program. The treasurer is responsible for deciding which financial underwriters are allowed to resell tax-exempt revenue bonds to investors. Because of this, financial firms often contribute heavily to the campaigns for treasurer.

## SECRETARY OF STATE

www.ss.ca.gov

The *SECRETARY OF STATE serves as the official record keeper of the acts of the legislature and the various executive departments and is the supervisor of all state elections*. He or she maintains the state archives and is the keeper of the Great Seal of California, which must be affixed to all documents signed by the governor. All businesses, counties, and cities are granted incorporation charters by the Secretary of State. Most importantly, the Secretary of State must: enforce the state's election laws, print state ballot pamphlets, certify and publish election results, and check for the proper number of signatures on petitions for initiative, referendum, and recall.

In addition, he or she must collect and approve statements of campaign donations and expenses. Many feel that the office of Secretary of State should be nonpartisan because of the intense involvement in the conducting of elections and the approval of campaign contributions.

### Chapter 6

## SUPERINTENDENT OF PUBLIC INSTRUCTION

www.cde.ca.gov/executive

The *SUPERINTENDENT OF PUBLIC INSTRUCTION is the director of the state Department of Education and is the only nonpartisan officer of the plural executive*. The Department of Education provides approximately 80% of the K-12 public school budget and sets standards for textbooks and curriculum. The Superintendent is "Director of the Department of Education," but the policies for the Department of Education are established by the ten-member State Board of Education, all of whom are appointed by the governor. The superintendent is the secretary of the board and is supposed to implement the rules and regulations it adopts.

## INSURANCE COMMISSIONER

www.insurance.ca.gov

The *INSURANCE COMMISSIONER is responsible for overseeing the massive California insurance industry, as a whole, and for the approval of all future auto insurance rate increases*. The office was changed from an appointed position to an elected one with the passage of Proposition 103.

The Insurance Commissioner's position was created by the voters to lower auto insurance rates, which had been rising faster than food costs for some people. The commissioner's role has since increased to cover a myriad of insurance issues in the state.

## STATE BOARD OF EQUALIZATION

www.boe.ca.gov

The *STATE BOARD OF EQUALIZATION is the five-member governmental body that is responsible for the assessment of all property in California*. The state is divided into 4 districts. An elected member from each district serves on the board along with the State Controller, who serves ex officio. *EX OFFICIO means that the holder of one office (State Controller) is automatically the holder of the second office (State Board of Equalization).*

The four Board of Equalization districts are:

| | |
|---|---|
| District One............ | Northern California |
| District Two............ | Central California |
| District Three........... | Central Los Angeles Area |
| District Four........... | South-Eastern California |

## The Executive Branch

 www.boe.ca.gov

The Board of Equalization is also responsible for collecting:

1. Sales tax,
2. Cigarette tax,
3. Gas tax,
4. Alcohol beverage tax, and
5. Other miscellaneous taxes.

## Recent Popular Governors

The following six governors were elected for at least two terms and deserve special recognition.

**Earl Warren "The Nonpartisan Advocate"**
**1943-1953 (three terms) Republican-Democrat**

Earl Warren was so popular that he is the only governor in California history elected for three terms. In his second term he won both the Republican and Democratic nominations under the old cross-filing system (which has since been abolished). He pushed for reforms in worker's compensation, prison conditions, and old-age pensions, but referred to them as progressive, not liberal ideas. He was appointed Chief Justice of the U.S. Supreme Court by President Dwight D. Eisenhower in 1953.

**Edmund "Pat" Brown "The First Brown"**
**1959-1966 (two terms) Democrat**

Edmund G. Brown faced controversy over the pressing state problems of water development, smog control, and capital punishment. By the end of his second term as governor, the state had greatly increased its spending. He more than doubled the miles of freeways, increased the State University and University of California Systems, and began the huge State Water Project.

**Ronald Reagan "The Conservative"**
**1967-1974 (two terms) Republican**

Ronald Reagan, a former actor, excellent speaker, and a conservative who did not like "big government spending," won the governorship easily. Although taxes and spending went up slightly while he was governor, he

**Chapter 6**

cut and trimmed the budget where he could. Reagan supported "law and order" but had trouble reforming welfare programs. His popularity carried him into the Presidency of the United States for two terms.

**Edmund "Jerry" Brown Jr. "The Non-traditionalist"**
**1975-1982 (two terms) Democrat**

Jerry Brown was a non-traditional governor, interested in the quality of life. Brown, an environmentalist, wanted alternative energy sources. He was against Proposition 13, the property tax reduction initiative, but supported it when it passed. That was the major factor in his landslide re-election in 1978.

**George Deukmejian "The Uninteresting Conservative"**
**1983-1990 (two terms) Republican**

"Duke," as the press called him, was a conservative who was mostly interested in keeping the cost of government down.

He took the responsibility of proposing a balanced budget very seriously. During his eight-year tenure as governor, he used his veto authority 4,000 times because the legislature was consistently trying to spend more money than was available.

**Pete Wilson "Growth Problem Handler"**
**1991-1999 (two terms) Republican**

Pete Wilson was a moderate republican who was on a mission to handle, or at least minimize, California's population growth problems. The challenge of increasing highway, school and prison construction, while trimming state funded services and increasing funding by raising taxes, did not win him any popularity contests.

Wilson believed California's growth pains must be solved or improved if we are to continue to accommodate the anticipated population growth and yet remain competitive. One of his priorities was keeping California businesses from leaving the state.

# The Executive Branch

## Governors of the State of California
## 1850-Present

1849-1851: Peter Burnett (Democrat)
1851-1852: John McDougall (Democrat)
1852-1856: John Bigler (Democrat)
1856-1858: J. Neeley Johnson (American)
1858-1860: John Weller (Democrat)
1860-1860: Milton Latham (Democrat)
1860-1862: John Downey (Democrat)
1862-1863: Leland Stanford (Republican)
1863-1867: Frederick Low (Unionist)
1867-1871: Henry Haight (Democrat)
1871-1875: Newton Booth (Republican)
      1875: Romualdo Pacheco (Republican, acting)
1875-1880: William Irwin (Democrat)
1880-1883: George Perkins (Republican)
1883-1887: George Stoneman (Democrat)
1887-1887: Washington Bartlett (Democrat)
1887-1891: Robert Waterman (Republican)
1891-1895: Henry Markham (Republican)
1895-1899: James Budd (Democrat)
1899-1903: Henry Gage (Republican)
1903-1907: George Pardee (Republican)
1907-1911: James Gillett (Republican)
1911-1918: Hiram W. Johnson (Republican)
1917-1923: William Stephens (Republican)
1923-1927: Friend Richardson (Republican)
1927-1931: C. C. Young (Republican)
1931-1934: James Rolph (Republican)
1934-1939: Frank Merriam (Republican)
1939-1943: Culburt Olson (Democrat)
1943-1953: Earl Warren (Republican)
1953-1959: Goodwin Knight (Republican)
1959-1967: Pat Brown (Democrat)
1967-1975: Ronald Reagan (Republican)
1975-1983: Jerry Brown (Democrat)
1983-1991: George Deukmejian (Republican)
1991-1999: Pete Wilson (Republican)
1999-2003: Gray Davis (Democrat) (First Recalled)
2003-present: Arnold Schwarzenegger (Republican)

# Chapter 6

## Chapter Summary

California has a "plural" executive branch, meaning that less power is concentrated in a single chief executive. The governor works with eleven other elected officials, each running a separate part of the government. Unlike the governor's appointees and cabinet members, these plural executives will often represent different political parties than the governor. They include the Lieutenant Governor, Attorney General, Controller, Secretary of State, Treasurer, Superintendent of Public Instruction, Insurance Commissioner, and the four members of the Board of Equalization.

Arnold Schwarzenegger, the Governor of California, has several important roles. He is the ceremonial leader of the state, greeting important dignitaries and representing California to the nation and the rest of the world. The governor is also the leader of his political party in California. He makes appointments to key state offices and commissions. The governor also nominates judges to the state supreme court, as well as filling vacancies on some of the lower courts. The governor has the power to grant clemency to convicted felons, giving full pardons, commuting a sentence, or granting reprieves. The governor is automatically the Commander-in-Chief of the state militia, calling the National Guard to active duty at will.

The governors most important responsibility is that of legislative leader. The governor's office prepares a state budget to accomplish these goals and submits it to the legislature for approval. The legislature makes its adjustments and passes the budget back in the form of an appropriations bill. The governor then has the option of approving the budget, or reducing and eliminating specific budget items by using the "line item veto."

The governor has veto power over any bill passed by the legislature. It takes a two-thirds vote of both the assembly and the senate to override a gubernatorial veto. If the governor signs a bill, it becomes law.

The lieutenant governor has few significant duties. The attorney general is legal counsel for the state and director of the justice department, responsible for the fair enforcement of California's laws. The state controller is the state's chief accountant and the chair of the Franchise Tax Board. The superintendent of public instruction, a nonpartisan post, directs the Department of Education. The secretary of state is California's official record-keeper, recording all acts of the legislature and overseeing elections. The state treasurer is responsible for supervising the bonds we issue to finance huge public works projects for the state. The insurance

## The Executive Branch

commissioner oversees the massive California insurance industry. The State Board of Equalization has four members plus the state controller. They are responsible for assessing real estate for tax purposes. They also collect sales taxes and taxes on cigarettes, gasoline, and alcohol.

## Class Discussion Questions

1. Which one of the plural executives has no daily assigned tasks and why?

2. Which of the plural executives positions was created by an initiative drive to cut the cost of owning an automobile?

3. How can the governor trim a budget bill without the help and cooperation of others?

4. Which of our recent governors served two or three terms?

5. Which one of our governors became Chief Justice of the U.S. Supreme Court? President of the United States?

# Chapter 7
# The California Legislature: Our Lawmakers

## LEGISLATURE (OUR LAWMAKERS)

The California Legislature, as the representative of the people, has the responsibility of making the laws and controlling the state's money. California has a **BICAMERAL** legislature. *It is made up of two houses: the state senate and the state assembly.* The state senate is referred to as the "upper house" and consists of only 40 members, and the state assembly is referred to as "lower house" and consists of 80 members.

## How the State Legislature Functions

 www.leginfo.ca.gov

The main purpose of the legislature is to enact bills that:

1. **SPEND THE STATE'S MONEY**
2. **ESTABLISH STATE TAXES**
3. **MAKE STATE LAWS**

The legislature also has other functions such as: redistricting, placing constitutional amendments on the ballot, oversight responsibilities and the conducting of confirmation hearings.

## LEGISLATIVE PROCESS

The legislative process in Sacramento begins with a bill. A *BILL is a draft of a law presented to the state senate or state assembly for approval or rejection.* Once a bill has been introduced by a member of one of the houses, it is sent to a legislative committee for study and revision. If it gains committee approval,

## Chapter 7

the bill is sent to the floor of that house for a vote by the entire membership. Eventually, a majority in each house must agree on the bill before it is sent to the governor.

### BILLS NEXT GO TO THE GOVERNOR

The governor, after receiving a bill, has 12 days in which to sign, not sign, or veto it. If the governor signs or does not take any action on the bill, it becomes law. If the governor vetoes the bill it is dead, unless two-thirds of the members in each house vote to override the veto.

### THE LEGISLATURE MAY OVERRIDE A VETO

The legislature may override the governor's veto. A *VETO OVERRIDE means that the legislature can make laws, even if the governor vetoes a bill, by obtaining the required two-thirds vote of the members in each house.* In recent history, Governor Edmund "Jerry" Brown Jr. (1975-1982) vetoed about 10% of all bills sent to him, causing a large number of veto overrides.

### LEGISLATIVE SESSIONS

The legislature meets in time periods referred to as sessions. The *GENERAL SESSION is a two-year period that starts at noon on the first Monday in December, during even-numbered years, and ends on November 30 of the next even-numbered year.* With the passage of the "term limits" initiative (two terms, eight years total for state senators and three terms, six years total for assembly members), the careers of legislators can best be described as "temporary full-time professionals."

### BUDGET BILL

Each year before January 11, the governor must submit a proposed budget for consideration to the senate and assembly. The budget bill must be enacted in both houses by midnight, on June 15, annually. This deadline has not always been met in the past.

A *SPECIAL SESSION can be called by the governor to deal with urgent matters.* Legislative action is limited to only the subject specified by the governor.

### REAPPORTIONMENT (NEXT REDISTRICTING IN 2012)

*REAPPORTIONMENT is the process of dividing districts into groups that are approximately equal in population.* This process is also called re-mapping, mapping, redistricting, or districting. The principle of equal-elective

# The California Legislature: Our Lawmakers

## THE FUNCTIONS OF THE CALIFORNIA STATE LEGISLATURE

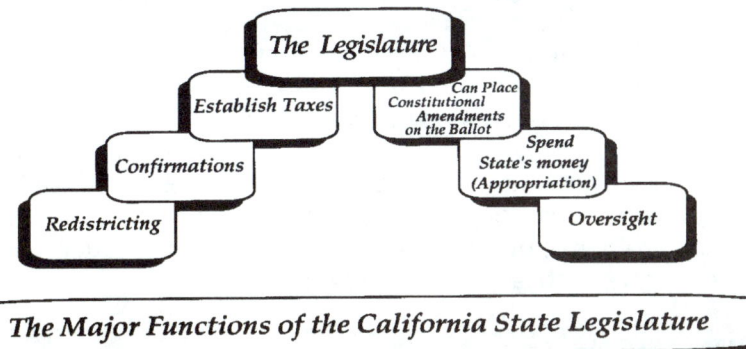

The Major Functions of the California State Legislature

  www.leginfo.ca.gov

representation requires districts to be redrawn at the beginning of each decade to conform to changes in population.

The legislature reapportions not only the state assembly, but the U.S. congressional districts and board of equalization districts.

The problem with having legislators do the reapportioning is that the majority party will naturally draw the district lines so that it will have the voter support advantage in elections. *GERRYMANDERING is the process of redrawing district lines to increase the number of seats held by the majority party.*

## CONSTITUTIONAL AMENDMENT

The legislature, by the passage of a constitutional amendment, was provided with a direct method of amending the state constitution. If two-thirds of the membership of each house concur, the legislature can submit a constitutional amendment directly to the people by simply placing it on the ballot where it must then be ratified by a majority of the voters.

## OVERSIGHT

Certain committees in the legislature perform an oversight function. *OVERSIGHT COMMITTEES act as watchdogs to make sure legislation, or programs that have been passed by the legislature, are being carried out properly by the employees of the executive branch. They also review the efficiency of programs to see if these programs can be accomplished more economically.*

**Chapter 7**

When an oversight committee's investigation reveals a severe impropriety, the state constitution allows the legislature to proceed with impeachment. *IMPEACHMENT is the process by which the legislature formally charges an elected official with misconduct.* The assembly must first vote for the articles of impeachment before they can be sent to the senate. The elected official is then tried in the senate where a two-thirds vote of the full membership is necessary to remove the official.

These severe measures, however, are rare. In general, oversight is not as exciting or glamorous for legislators as introducing bills or handling constituency problems, but it is a vital function of a bureaucracy in order to help make for an effective and efficient government.

## CONFIRMATIONS

*CONFIRMATION is the process in the state senate of either approving or rejecting, by a majority vote, the hundreds of appointments made by the governor.* Confirmation hearings are held for the heads of the governor's cabinet, commissions, boards, and even the director of the Department of Motor Vehicles. The senate rules committee holds hearings on the fitness of all the nominees and makes a recommendation to the full membership of the senate. If the full senate approves a candidate by a simple majority vote, the candidate is confirmed. The assembly does not play an active role in the confirmation process, although the candidate does need a two-thirds approval vote from the assembly as well as the senate.

*California Senate*

www.sen.ca.gov

## CALIFORNIA SENATE (UPPER HOUSE)

The *CALIFORNIA SENATE is the upper house in the legislature with 40 members serving four year-terms (two term limit), with half of the senate districts conducting elections every two years.* The U.S. Supreme Court requires the upper house of a state legislature to be based on population rather than the geographic size of the county. This has resulted in a shift of more senate seats to Southern California.

The senate has, for many years, been more stable, less partisan, and more conservative in its procedures than the assembly. Each senator represents over 887,500 people. The number of senators has been set by the state constitution at 40, exactly half the size of the state assembly.

# The California Legislature: Our Lawmakers

## SENATE LEADERSHIP

According to our state constitution, the **LIEUTENANT GOVERNOR** *is automatically the president of the senate but, in actuality, this is largely a ceremonial post*. He or she has no role of note in senate matters unless there is a rare 20-20 vote, then the lieutenant governor provides the tie-breaking vote.

The powerful **SENATE PRESIDENT PRO TEMPORE** *is the member elected by the senate to be its leader*. Since the lieutenant governor is rarely present during most sessions, the leadership of the upper house is vested in the Senate President Pro Tempore. Chosen by fellow senators, the "Pro Tem" is the one who presides over the senate.

The **SENATE RULES COMMITTEE** *is chaired by the Senate President Pro Tempore, and includes four other members elected by the senate*. This committee has the power to appoint all the other senate committee chairs and vice-chairs. The senate rules committee is also extremely powerful in that it decides which committee will be assigned to each bill coming up for consideration. It also selects the senators who will serve on executive and judicial boards and commissions.

The **MAJORITY AND MINORITY FLOOR LEADERS** *are senate members appointed by their party to direct the party's political strategy in the legislature*.

## THE PRESTIGE OF THE SENATE

The senate chamber is decorated in deep reds—the traditional color of the upper class—and with good reason. The "upper house," with its small number of representatives and longer term, is more select—and, therefore, more prestigious—than the assembly. If an assembly member has a chance to win election to the senate, he or she will usually do so. But now that we have term limitations, don't be surprised if you see senate members switch to the assembly—and visa-versa—just to remain in the legislature for a few more terms.

## California Assembly

www.assembly.ca.gov

## THE CALIFORNIA ASSEMBLY (LOWER HOUSE)

The **CALIFORNIA STATE ASSEMBLY** *is the lower house in the legislature with 80 members serving two-year terms (three term limit)*. The assembly is known for its power struggles and is generally more volatile than the senate.

### Chapter 7

## ASSEMBLY LEADERSHIP

The powerful *SPEAKER OF THE ASSEMBLY is the presiding officer of the assembly, elected by the membership and automatically serving (ex officio) on all assembly and joint legislative committees.* His or her powers parallel those of the president pro tempore, the counterpart in the senate. The speaker names a member of his or her political party to be the majority floor leader. But the entire assembly elects an *ASSEMBLY SPEAKER PRO TEMPORE, who runs the proceedings during the speaker's absence.* The speaker also chairs the assembly's rules committee. This important position allows the speaker to control the flow of legislative activity on the floor—in much the same way that the senate's rules committee chair (the pro tem) controls the legislative business of that house.

The *MAJORITY PARTY FLOOR LEADER is appointed by the speaker to represent the majority party.* The *MINORITY PARTY FLOOR LEADER is chosen by, and represents, the minority party.* The minority floor leader is also called the "minority whip."

## Committee System

The legislature does all of its work by the use of the committee system. A *COMMITTEE SYSTEM is a system whereby the legislature is broken down into smaller committees; a basic working component that can study all bills in depth.* Most new bills are first referred to one of the standing committees for in-depth study and review.

## THE DIFFERENT TYPES OF COMMITTEES

The *RULES COMMITTEES are powerful committees that refer all bills to standing committees, as well as selecting and supervising the assembly support staff.* It is chaired in the senate by the pro tem, and in the assembly by the speaker.

*STANDING COMMITTEES are the basic, or core, committees that will do most of the work for the current session and are established by the rules of each house at the beginning of each session.* There are currently 28 established standing committees in the assembly and 25 in the senate. Good old-fashioned politics determines who controls these committees and what the exact membership will be during each session. Each committee is assigned bills, according to its jurisdiction, which it will hear, study, hold public hearings on, change as needed, and finally vote on in committee.

# The California Legislature: Our Lawmakers

## Requirements for Legislators

**ELIGIBILITY...** At least 18 years of age.

**RESIDENCY...** California resident for three years, at least one year in the district (immediately prior).

**TERM LIMIT...** Two, four-year terms for the senate (8 years) and three, two-year terms (6 years) for the assembly.

**SENATE SEAT ROTATION...** 20 seats each even-numbered year.

**ASSEMBLY SEAT ROTATION...** All 80 seats even-numbered years.

**CODE OF ETHICS...** Binds both houses—may expel a member by two-thirds vote.

**COMPENSATION...** $99,000 salary and $121 per day living expenses when in session. Telephone and gasoline expense allowance for a state-licensed automobile. Limited health and retirement benefits.

In addition to the standing committees in each house, the legislature also employs joint committees. *JOINT COMMITTEES are committees consisting of an equal number of assembly members and senators who study subjects of mutual interest to both houses.* They recommend legislation that they believe will be acceptable to both houses.

*FISCAL COMMITTEES are standing financial committees that oversee the annual state budget and handle all other bills that either directly or indirectly involve a cost to the state.*

*CONFERENCE COMMITTEES are set up to resolve differences between the assembly and the senate versions of the same bill.*

*SELECT OR SPECIAL COMMITTEES are set up by either house to research limited subject areas where the forming of a permanent standing committee may not be seen as necessary.*

## LEGISLATORS' SALARY AND BENEFITS

Both chambers of the California Legislature receive the same base salary of $99,000 a year and, when the legislature is in session, a $121 tax free per day (per diem) living expense allowance. Six legislative leaders receive a larger salary because of their additional responsibilities. All legislators receive round-trip travel expenses to and from legislative sessions and

Chapter 7

### ASSEMBLY STANDING COMMITTEES

Aging and Long-Term Care
Agriculture
Appropriations
Arts, Entertainment, Sports, Tourism, and Internet Media
Banking and Finance
Budget
Business and Professions
Education
Elections, Redistricting, and Constitutional Amendments
Environmental Safety and Toxic Materials
Governmental Organization
Health
Higher Education
Housing and Community Development
Human Services
Insurance
Judiciary
Labor and Employment
Local Government
Natural Resources
Public Employees, Retirement, and Social Security
Public Safety
Revenue and Taxation
Rules
Transportation
Utilities and Commerce
Veterans Affairs
Water, Parks, and Wildlife

committee meetings, gas and telephone credit cards, and use of a state-licensed auto. This salary, including perks, makes them the highest paid legislators in the country.

## *Types of Legislation*

### (BILLS AND RESOLUTIONS)

There are basically two types of legislation: bills and resolutions. The most important type, as discussed earlier, is a bill. Most of the work done by the legislature is expressed in the form of bills. The state budget and state taxes are no exception. New budgets and taxes are discussed, revised, and approved or rejected as bills. The majority of California's bills pass through the legislature according to the procedure described in "Legislative Process." Two special kinds of bills, however, follow different rules.

An *APPROPRIATION BILL* *is one that authorizes funds to be spent from state revenues.* *URGENT BILLS* *are bills that must take effect immediately after being enacted.* These two types of bills require a two-thirds approval of each house.

Bills are assigned numbers so that they can be identified easily. Assembly bills have an (AB) before each number and (SB) is placed before a senate bill.

## The California Legislature: Our Lawmakers

> ### Term Limits... Proposition 140
>
> Proposition 140 is called the Term Limits Initiative, but after changes made by a federal court, it only does the following:
>
> 1. Limits the terms of state senators to two (eight total years);
> 2. Limits the terms of assembly members to three (six total years); and
> 3. Limits the terms of governor and other state elected officials to two (eight total years).
>
> Californians see term limitations for officeholders as a first step in making the political system more responsive to new people, new programs, and change!
>
> **U.S. Congressional members from California have no term limits.**

The second type of legislation is the resolution. A *RESOLUTION is a vote on a matter that involves one house, or in some instances both the assembly and senate, but does not require the governor's approval.* There are four kinds of resolutions:

**CONSTITUTIONAL AMENDMENT** – known as ACA or SCA, depending on the house of origination. A constitutional amendment is a resolution to change our state's constitution. An amendment must pass by a two-thirds majority in each house before it can be placed on the next election ballot. It must be ratified by a majority of those voting before the constitution can be changed.

**CONCURRENT RESOLUTION** – known as ACR or SCR, depending on the house of origination. This is used to adopt joint rules, establish joint committees, and congratulate groups or individuals. A simple majority of each house is needed to pass a concurrent resolution.

**JOINT RESOLUTION** – known as AJR or SJR, depending on the house of origination. This action urges the U.S. congress to pass or defeat legislation currently before it. In this way the state legislature lets its opinion be known regarding national issues.

**HOUSE RESOLUTION** – known as AR or SR, depending on the house of origination. A house resolution is used to create one-term committees, amend rules of that house, and congratulate groups and individuals. These resolutions are usually adopted by a voice vote of the majority.

### Chapter 7

## TRACKING LEGISLATION (BILLS)

A person can receive a free copy of a current bill, as it goes through the legislature, by simply going to the "bill room" in the basement of the state capitol building in Sacramento.

With the huge number of bills introduced in each two-year legislative session, both houses publish guides to help keep interested people informed. The *DAILY FILE is an agenda of that day's business*, whereas the *DAILY JOURNAL contains an account of the preceding day.*

In addition to these guides, histories are published by each house. There is *DAILY HISTORY, WEEKLY HISTORY, SEMIFINAL HISTORY*, a *FINAL HISTORY* and a *LEGISLATIVE INDEX* of the entire two-year legislative session. These all summarize the actions taken on bills during this period.

## *Legislative Staff*

### EMPLOYEES

The legislature of California has one of the largest staffs in the United States. Each legislative member is entitled to an administrative assistant and secretaries for both his or her capital office and also the district office.

### JOINT STAFF

The *LEGISLATIVE COUNSEL (www.leginfo.ca.gov) is the chief legal counsel for the legislature, which is selected at the beginning of each session by the agreement of both houses*. Most bills are prepared by the legislative counsel's office. This counsel advises the legislature on the legality and constitutionality of measures and prepares indexes of the California codes and statutes.

The *LEGISLATIVE ANALYST (www.lao.ca.gov) provides the legislature with financial, economic, and fiscal advice. He or she is appointed by the joint legislative budget committee.* The staff of the legislative analyst's office evaluates every item in the proposed state budget and all bills (appropriation bills) requiring money that go before the fiscal (revenue and expenditure) committee. Most importantly, the legislative analyst prepares a financial analysis of each proposition to be included in the state ballot pamphlet.

The *AUDITOR GENERAL is appointed by the joint legislative audit committee to assist the legislature by examining, auditing, and reporting on the financial statements submitted by the executive branch.*

# The California Legislature: Our Lawmakers

## Media Coverage

### CAL-SPAN

The California assembly (lower house) televises its proceedings live on cable television. CAL-SPAN is the nonprofit company that distributes the signal to a statewide cable system available to over two million subscribers.

### C-SPAN—NATIONAL COVERAGE

C-SPAN, the nation's television programmer for the federal government, is very successful. It is so successful that it broadcasts "full-time coverage" of all types of events that are affected by federal policy. Its reports are entirely objective and nonpartisan.

### NEWSPAPERS AND NEWS SERVICES

Californians are kept up-to-date on political news from Sacramento by reading newspapers and periodicals, listening to the radio, and watching network programming or cable coverage. Since Sacramento, the capital, is the political news center, many newspapers, news services, magazines, and newsletters maintain capital bureaus.

## State Newspapers

- Alameda Times-Star
- Modoc County Record (Alturas)
- The Arcata Eye
- Times Press Recorder (Arroyo Grande)
- Auburn Journal
- Bakersfield Californian
- Desert Dispatch (Barstow)
- Benicia News
- Daily Planet (Berkeley)
- East Bay Express
- Beverly Hills Weekly
- Big Bear Grizzly
- Valley Times (Palo Verde)
- The Desert Independent
- Carmel Pine Cone
- Carmichael Times Newspaper
- Coastal View News (Carpenteria)
- Enterprise-Record (Chico)
- Chico Examiner
- Chico News & Review
- Rabbit Creek Journal (Clipper Mills)
- Coalinga's Own
- Oange County Weekly
- The Daily Triplicate
- Crestline Courier-News
- Crestline Chronicle
- Cupertino Courier
- Davis Enterprise
- Independent Voice (Dixon)
- Press Online (Imperial Valley)
- Citizen (Elk Grove)
- North County Times
- Times-Standard (Eureka)
- Daily Republic (Fairfield)
- Valley Banner (Felton Scotts)
- Telegraph (Folsom)
- Herald News (Fontana)
- Advocate-News (Fort Bragg)
- Fresno Bee
- The Galt Herald
- The Gilroy Dispatch
- The Union
- Half Moon Bay Review
- Hanford Sentinel
- The Valley Chronicle
- Free Lance (Hollister)
- Pinnacle News (Hollister)
- Huntington Beach News
- Idyllwild Town Crier
- Irvine World News
- Kingsburg Recorder
- Valley Sun (La Canada)
- Lake Arrowhead Mountain News
- Kern Valley Sun (Lake Isabella)
- Lake County Record-Bee
- The Independent (Livermore)
- Lodi News-Sentinel
- Lompoc Record
- Grunion Gazette (Long Beach)
- Long Beach Press-Telegram
- Lompoc Record
- City News (Los Angeles)
- Investor's Business Daily (Los Angeles)
- Jewish Observer (Los Angeles)
- La Opinion (Los Angeles)
- L.A. Weekly
- Los Angeles Daily News
- Los Angeles Downtown News
- Los Angeles Times
- Los Banos Enterprise
- Los Gatos Daily News
- Los Gatos Weekly-Times
- Madera Tribune
- Malibu Times
- Lake Mammoth Times
- Manteca Bulletin
- The Argonaut (Marina del Rey)
- Marysville Appeal-Democrat
- The Mendocino Beacon
- The Almanac (Menlo Park)
- Sun-Star (Merced)
- Modesto Bee
- Monterey County Herald
- Morgan Hill Times
- Mount Shasta Herald
- Napa Valley Register
- Orange County Business Journal
- Marin Independent Journal
- Novato Advance
- Sierra Star (Oakhurst)
- Ojai Valley News
- East Bay Express (Oakland)
- Oakland Tribune
- Inland Valley Daily Bulletin (Ontario)
- Orange County Register
- Mercury-Register (Oroville)
- Palisadian-Post (Pacific Palisades)
- Pacifica Tribune
- The Desert Sun (Palm Springs)
- Antelope Valley Press (Palmdale)
- Daily News (Palo Alto)
- The Daily Republican (Palo Alto)
- Palo Alto Online

Paradise Post
Pasadena Star-News
Argus-Courier (Petaluma)
Mountain Democrat (Placerville)
Business Times (Pleasanton)
Tri-Valley Herald (Pleasanton)
Point Reyes Light
Recorder (Porterville)
Pomerado Newspaper (Poway)
Feather River Bulletin (Quincy)
Ramona Sentinel
Rancho Cucamonga Business Journal
Daily News (Red Bluff)
Record Searchlight (Redding)
Daily Facts (Redlands)
The Daily Independent (Ridgecrest)
Riverside Press-Enterprise
Community Voice (Rohnert Park)
The Press Tribune (Roseville)
Alpenhorn News (Running Springs)
Sacramento Bee
Sacramento Business Journal
Sacramento News & Review
Star (Saint Helena)
The Californian (Salinas)
Calaveras Enterprise (San Andreas)
Calaveras Publishing Co
County Sun (San Bernardino)
San Diego Community Newspaper Group
Daily Transcript (San Diego)
La Prensa (San Diego)
San Diego Headline News
Union-Tribune (San Diego)
Reader (San Diego)
Coast News (San Diego)
Business Times (San Francisco)
El Observador (San Francisco)
San Francisco Chronicle
San Francisco Examinier
San Francisco Guardian
San Francisco Weekly
San Gabriel Tribune
San Jose Mercury News
Metro (San Jose)
Business Journal (San Jose)
Willow Glen Resident (San Jose)
New Times Weekly (San Luis Obispo)
Telegram-Tribune (San Luis Obispo)
County Times (San Mateo)
Daily Journal (San Mateo)
Marin Independant Journal (San Rafael)
Orange County Register (Santa Ana)
Independent (Santa Barbara)
News Press (Santa Barbara)
The South Coast Beacon

The Signal (Santa Clarita)
Good Times (Santa Cruz)
Metro (Santa Cruz)
Santa Cruz Sentinel
Santa Maria Sun
Santa Maria Times
Santa Monica Mirror
Santa Paula Times
The Press Democrat (Santa Rosa)
Bay Business Journal
Saratoga News
Scotts Valley Banner
Coast Weekly (Seaside)
Sebastopol Times and News
Enterprise (Selma)
Index-Tribune (Sonoma)
Union Democrat (Sonora)
Tahoe Daily Tribune
The Record (Stockton)
Sun (Sunnyvale)
Lassen County Times (Susanville)
Tahoe Daily Tribune
Tahoe World
Tehachapi News
The Ark (Tiburon)
Messenger (Topanga)
Daily Breeze (Torrance)
Press (Tracy)
Sierra Sun (Truckee)
Advance-Register (Tulare)
The Desert Trail (Twenty-Nine Palms)
Daily Journal (Ukiah)
The Reporter (Vacaville)
VallejoNews.com (Vallejo)
Times-Herald (Vallejo)
Valley Roadrunner (Valley Center)
Star Ventura (Ventura County)
The Daily Press (Victorville)
Times-Delta (Visalia)
North Bay Business Journal (Walnut Creek)
Contra Costa Times (Walnut Creek)
Register-Pajaronian (Watsonville)
San Gabriel Valley Tribune
Daily News (Whittier)
The Daily Democrat (Woodland)
Los Angeles Daily News (Woodland Hills)
Siskiyou Daily News (Yreka)
Hi-Desert Star (Yucca Valley)

www.usnpl.com/canews.html

# Chapter 7

## Chapter Summary

The California state legislature is patterned after the national legislature in Washington, D.C. It is a "bicameral" legislature that consists of two houses: the state senate and the state assembly. The senate (or upper house) has forty members. The assembly (or lower house) has eighty. Bills are drafts of proposed legislative action. They are used by the legislature to create new laws, approve the spending of money, or to permit the legislature to raise money through taxes. A bill must be approved by a majority of both houses before it can be passed on to the governor for approval. Certain bills and resolutions (such as appropriations bills, urgent bills, and constitutional amendments) require a two-thirds majority vote in each house to be approved. Resolutions are legislative votes on matters that do not require the governor's approval.

Senate members serve four-year terms and assembly members serve two-year terms. Under term limitations (Prop. 140), senators may serve for eight years (two terms) while assembly members serve for no more than six years (three terms). To hold a legislative seat, a person must be at least 18 years old and be a California resident for at least three years (living in the represented district for at least one year).

With only forty members, the state senate (or upper house) is more prestigious than the assembly. Each senator represents more than 887,500 citizens. The lieutenant governor is the ceremonial president of the senate, but the real leader is the senate president pro tempore. The pro tem is elected by the senate and is the counterpart to the speaker of the assembly. He or she controls the flow of legislation, makes important committee appointments, and chairs the powerful senate rules committee (comparable to the rules committee in the assembly). The pro tem controls the purse strings of the state, since the rules committee must approve all expenditures. Each party also appoints a majority or minority floor leader.

The presiding officer of the assembly is the speaker. The speaker is elected by the members, and serves on all joint legislative committees. This very powerful position dominates the legislature, controlling the flow of legislative activity, controlling the size and membership of all the committees, and appointing committee chairs and other important posts. The speaker appoints the majority party floor leader to represent his or her party during the session. The minority party also has its own floor leader. A speaker pro tempore (or pro tem) is selected by the membership to run the day-to-day proceedings. The pro tem is an automatic member of the powerful assembly rules committee, but has no vote. The assembly rules

## The California Legislature: Our Lawmakers

committee is chaired by the speaker. It controls the flow of all bills through the assembly and also supervises the assembly support staff.

Each legislative session lasts two years, starting the first Monday in December on even numbered years and ending two years later on November 30. Every year the governor must submit a proposed budget by January 11. The legislature is required to work with the governor's budget and both houses must enact it by June 15. The governor calls a "special session" of the legislature to deal with a specific urgent matter.

Another difficult responsibility for the state legislature is reapportionment of the state assembly and the U.S. congressional districts. The next one takes effect in 2012.

## Class Discussion Questions

1. What does the state legislature do for us?

2. Why does a state senator have "more prestige"?

3. Why do the assembly speaker and the senate president pro tempore have so much power?

4. What is the difference between a bill and a resolution?

5. Term limitations had what effect on the legislators?

# Chapter 8
## Our Judicial System

 www.courtinfo.ca.gov

Most Californians have little direct contact with the state's judicial system, except for the occasional traffic ticket, but this system of courts is an essential part of our government.

### JUSTICE IS PRIMARILY A "STATE ACTIVITY"

The *CALIFORNIA JUDICIAL SYSTEM* is the branch of the state government that administers justice under the law. Unlike many other government operations, the judicial system is run primarily by the state. Ninety percent of all court cases filed in California are handled by our state courts. Federal law violations and state law claims which depend on some element of federal law can be heard in federal courts.

Our California judicial system, as a whole, is considered conservative. It consists primarily of our courts, but is supported by a network of agencies and departments working together. This network—representing not just the judicial branch, but the executive and legislative branches as well—includes the following groups:

1. Three-Level Court Structure
2. Court-related Commissions and the Judicial Council
3. Attorneys and the State Bar Association
4. Peace Officers
5. Participating Citizens
6. Correction and Rehabilitation Agencies

### Chapter 8

# *California's Three-Level Court Structure*

California's judicial power is vested in three courts:

1. Superior Court
2. Court of Appeal
3. Supreme Court

## COURTS: EITHER TRIAL OR APPELLATE COURTS

The three-tier court system can be divided into two types of courts: trial and appellate. A *TRIAL COURT is a local court where the facts are determined and a decision is made by a judge (or jury, if requested).* Superior Courts are primarily trial courts, but can also serve as Appellate Courts in certain situations. An *APPELLATE COURT determines whether the proper procedures were used in the original trial and whether the law was properly applied or interpreted.* The Court of Appeal generally hears cases on appeal. The Supreme Court has discretion to review Court of Appeal decisions.

All courts hear both civil and criminal cases.

*CIVIL CASES relate to individual rights and usually seek monetary damages.* The party filing a civil action is called the *PLAINTIFF* and the party defending is called the *DEFENDANT*. A *JUDGMENT states the amount of money awarded for damages by the judge or jury to the winner in a civil court case.*

*CRIMINAL CASES are brought by the State of California to punish violations of criminal laws.*

## SUPERIOR COURTS

At least one *SUPERIOR COURT is located in each county. It is the state's basic civil and criminal trial court.* The court's case load is made up mainly of:

1. Civil cases and personal injury cases.
2. Family law cases.
3. Guardianship cases.
4. Probate cases.

The Superior Court civil cases are divided into two categories; those which seek more than $25,000 (unlimited), and those that seek less than $25,000 (limited).

# Our Judicial System

Only about 25% of the cases are felony criminal cases—which must carry a possible jail term of a year or more—or juvenile delinquency problems.

*SMALL CLAIMS COURTS are small courts for civil cases where the amount in question is $5,000 or less.* The purpose of the Small Claims Court is to provide a speedy, inexpensive, informal method of settling claims without attorneys or usual legal procedure.

 www.courtinfo.ca.gov/courts/trial/smallclaims

## COURT OF APPEAL

The *COURT OF APPEAL primarily reviews trial court decisions for legal error.* Like the Supreme Court, they only hear cases that deal with the legal interpretation of a lower court decision. There are six districts of the Court of Appeal.

## THE CALIFORNIA SUPREME COURT

The *CALIFORNIA SUPREME COURT decides to review important questions of law to maintain statewide uniformity of legal decisions.* It has discretion to review Courts of Appeal decisions, which the parties petition to be reviewed. All death row cases are automatically appealed to the Supreme Court for review. It is made up of seven justices—the chief justice and six associate justices—and is the highest court in the state. A decision from this court is binding on all the other courts in California. When the Supreme Court wants to rule on a matter quickly, it can remove a case from a lower court and hear it directly.

## JUSTICES FACE ELECTION AFTER APPOINTMENT

After the justices of the State Supreme Court and the State Court of Appeal are appointed by the governor, they must be confirmed by the Commission on Judicial Appointments and then be voted on by the public at the next gubernatorial election. If the voters approve the governor's appointment, the justice continues in that position for a 12-year term after which he or she can once again run for another 12-year term. In addition, all Superior Court judges, if appointed to fill emergency vacancies, must run for the balance of their terms at the next regularly scheduled gubernatorial election. They must then run for re-election at the end of each term.

In an effort to keep political bias out of our courts, all judges in California are elected on a nonpartisan ballot.

*Chapter 8*

# California's Three-Level Court Structure

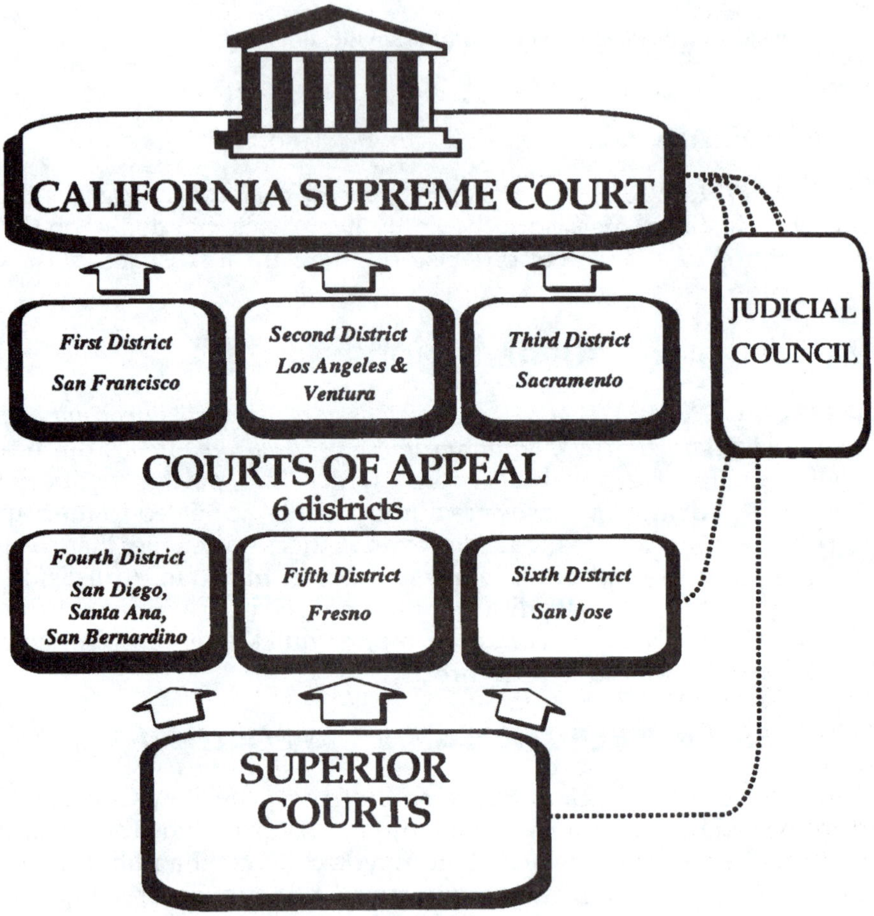

**CALIFORNIA SUPREME COURT**

*First District*
San Francisco

*Second District*
Los Angeles &
Ventura

*Third District*
Sacramento

**JUDICIAL COUNCIL**

**COURTS OF APPEAL**
6 districts

*Fourth District*
San Diego,
Santa Ana,
San Bernardino

*Fifth District*
Fresno

*Sixth District*
San Jose

**SUPERIOR COURTS**

*Our Judicial System*

## Commissions and the Judicial Council

The integrity and efficiency of California's court system is protected by three commissions and one council. They are the:

1. Commission on Judicial Appointments (Court of Appeal and Supreme Court)
2. Commission on Judicial Nominees (Superior Court)
3. Commission on Judicial Performance (Judicial discipline)
4. Judicial Council (Judicial administration)

### CONFIRMATION: HIGHER COURT JUSTICES

The *COMMISSION ON JUDICIAL APPOINTMENTS consists of three members who must confirm all judicial nominees for the California Courts of Appeal and Supreme Court.* The three members of the Commission on Judicial Appointments are: the Chief Justice of the State Supreme Court, the Attorney General of California and a senior presiding Justice of a District Court of Appeal. Their job is to hold hearings where law enforcement officials, members of the state bar, and private citizens can express their opinions or concerns about qualifications of the chosen nominee.

### NOMINATIONS: LOWER COURT JUSTICES

The governor also appoints judges to fill vacancies on the lower courts. The *COMMISSION ON JUDICIAL NOMINEES assists the evaluation of potential trial court judges, and must submit a report to the governor whether the nominee is qualified or not.* It is a 25-member commission appointed by the board of governors of the State Bar of California (a private association of attorneys). The governor can appoint any nominee he or she desires, but traditionally will not oppose the commission's recommendations.

### COMMISSION ON JUDICIAL PERFORMANCE

The *COMMISSION ON JUDICIAL PERFORMANCE is a commission of nine private citizens that investigates complaints of judicial misconduct or incapacity and disciplines judges.* The commission on judicial performance can recommend forced retirement or removal of any judge.

Chapter 8

## THE JUDICIAL COUNCIL

The *JUDICIAL COUNCIL has the responsibility of improving the adminstration of justice and for adopting rules for court administration, practice, and procedure.* The council oversees the business operations of our state courts and reports its recommendations for improvement to the legislature and the governor. In addition, the council addresses issues of racism, sexism, and language bias (against non-English speakers) in the courts. But most importantly, it plans for the future of the court system and its sources of funding.

## REMOVING A JUDGE

In California, there are four ways to remove a judge:

1. Normal election process.
2. Impeachment and conviction by the state legislature.
3. Recall election—called if 20% of the registered voters sign a recall petition.
4. Convicted of a felony or moral turpitude—must be recommended by commission on judicial performance.

## CALIFORNIA AND THE U.S. SUPREME COURT

 www.uscourts.gov

Usually, the U.S. Supreme Court may only hear a case litigated in a lower federal court or in a state court if it involves an issue of federal law. The U.S. Supreme Court also determines whether a state constitution or state law conforms to the provisions of the federal constitution. The state courts are bound by its decisions. In most states, cases must go through the state Supreme Court before being submitted to the U.S. Supreme Court. In California, however, cases may also go to the U.S. Supreme Court directly from a California Court of Appeal.

# *Court Procedures*

## CRIMINAL CASES

After being arrested, the accused is brought before a judge, usually a Superior Court judge, to be arraigned. An *ARRAIGNMENT is the court procedure where the judge officially informs accused parties of their legal rights and the charges against*

# Our Judicial System

*them.* The judge sets the date at the preliminary hearing and determines bail. ***BAIL*** *is the amount of money that must be posted before a person can be released from jail. If the accused is of little danger to the public, he or she can be released without bail, or, "on his or her **OWN RECOGNIZANCE**."*

Most criminal cases are resolved without a trial. Since trials are costly and time-consuming, the courts encourage plea bargaining. ***PLEA BARGAINING*** *is a negotiated agreement between the prosecutor and the defense attorney to accept a plea of guilty to a lesser crime than the defendant was originally accused of.*

In order to establish clear guidelines for punishment, crimes are grouped into three major categories: infractions, misdemeanors, and felonies. ***INFRACTIONS*** *are the least serious types of crimes, such as traffic violations. The punishment for an infraction is usually a fine and, in rare cases, jail time.* ***MISDEMEANORS*** *are more serious crimes, including such acts as drunk driving or shoplifting. Misdemeanor convictions carry fines and jail time of less than one year in prison.* ***FELONIES*** *are the most serious types of crimes and include such crimes as grand theft auto, drug trafficking, and murder. These crimes are punishable by prison terms of over a year and, under special circumstances, death.*

An alternative to prison terms is probation. ***PROBATION*** *is the act of suspending the sentence of a convicted offender and giving the offender supervised freedom.*

## JUVENILE OFFENDERS

***JUVENILES*** *are people under the age of 18 and, because of this fact, are treated differently from adults in our legal system.*

Our society wants to protect the juvenile and itself at the same time. A juvenile is not sent to jail or prison, but rather to juvenile hall until his or her case is heard and, if convicted, will be sent to a detention center where society will try to rehabilitate that person.

## CIVIL CASES

In a civil cases, the procedure is simpler. The plaintiff files a complaint with the court clerk. A ***COMPLAINT*** *is the legal charge or charges brought against the defendant.* The court then issues a summons for the defendant. The general procedures which follow issuance of the summons are: 1) the complaint is served on the defendant; 2) the defendant answers the complaint; 3) the parties engage in the discovery process to evaluate each other's evidence;

Chapter 8

## "Three Strikes"

The three strike law ensures that a person who commits certain serious or violent felonies will be given an increased prison sentence and greater punishment. It includes as prior convictions certain felonies committed by older juveniles. The stated purpose of the law is to curb repeat criminal activity. Here's how it works:

Strike One: One serious/violent felony serves as a first strike toward a stiffer prison term.

Strike Two: A second felony conviction, with one prior serious/violent felony, DOUBLES the base sentence for the conviction. No probation.

Strike three: A third felony conviction, with two serious/violent prior felonies, TRIPLES the base sentence or imposes 25 years to life, whichever is greater. No probation.

In March 2003, the United States Supreme Court upheld California's three strikes law. The court held that enhanced sentences served California's legitimate goal of deterring and incapacitating repeat offenders. It rejected the claim that the enhanced sentences were grossly disproportionate under the cruel and unusual punishment provisions of the Eighth Amendment of the Bill of Rights.

and 4) the case is either settled or tried before a judge or a jury, which decides the merits of the case.

## Attorneys and the State Bar

### CITIZENS' RIGHT TO AN ATTORNEY

The California Constitution and the U.S. Constitution both provide that a person accused of a crime has the right to be represented by an attorney.

### STATE BAR ASSOCIATION

 www.calbar.org

No person can practice law without first being admitted to the state bar. The **STATE BAR OF CALIFORNIA** *is the professional organization that is*

# Our Judicial System

## State Supreme Court Talks to Governor Schwarzenegger

The California Supreme Court is now dominated by conservatives who are less willing than previous justices to expand the peoples' rights beyond the scope of the state constitution. The court does not actively seek to extend state constitutional protections.

Chief Justice Ronald George met with Governor Arnold Schwarzenegger following the special election. The Governor showed an appreciation for the importance of the judicial branch, which includes:

1. 1,600 judges,
2. 19,000 court employees, and
3. $2.6 billion annual budget.

*authorized by the state constitution to admit candidates to practice law in California, set ethical standards, and discipline and expel attorneys.*

### PROSECUTING AND DEFENSE ATTORNEYS

The ***DISTRICT ATTORNEY (D.A.)*** *is the prosecuting attorney for the government at the county level.* He or she evaluates the cases brought before the D.A.'s office and decides which cases should be filed and go to trial.

As discussed earlier, few criminal cases actually go to trial. The cost to the judicial system would be astronomical if every criminal case did. In most instances the district attorney will drop up to half of all felony charges and only prosecute the stongest cases where there is good, factual evidence.

The ***DEFENSE ATTORNEY*** *is the attorney for the defendant.* A ***PUBLIC DEFENDER*** *is a county-employed attorney who represents the defendant in a criminal case when the defendant cannot afford private counsel.* Legal services for the indigent are also offered by such groups as Legal Aid.

Chapter 8

# Peace Officers

A **POLICE OFFICER** *is employed by a city and sworn to uphold justice.* The bulk of law enforcement work by the police is carried out at the street level. City police chiefs are usually appointed by the city manager or the police commission. The police officer's counterpart in the unincorporated county areas is called a sheriff's deputy.

A **SHERIFF** *is a peace officer who works for the county, runs the county jail, and provides a crime lab for the city police within that county if needed.* The County Sheriff, the top administrative officer, is elected through a nonpartisan election.

A **HIGHWAY PATROL OFFICER** *(www.chp.ca.gov) is a state peace officer who protects our safety on highways and state or county roads.*

The job of the **STATE POLICE** *is to protect state buildings, the governor, and other state officials.*

A **MARSHAL** *is a county peace officer who runs the courtrooms, serves court-related legal papers, and physically evicts tenants if ordered.* His or her main job is to protect the judges.

# Citizens' Participation

Citizens can participate in the judicial system as witnesses, jury members, or grand jury members.

A **WITNESS** *is an individual who has seen something relevant to the commission of a crime.*

In a **JURY TRIAL**, *a group of 12 men and women (or less) judges whether the accused (in a criminal case) is innocent or guilty of the charges, and in a civil case, which party prevails.* In civil trials, the number of jurors is reduced to eight if the parties stipulate to it. Jury members are selected from the county voter registration roll and DMV records.

Every county has a grand jury. A **GRAND JURY** *is a group of 19 citizens (23 in Los Angeles) who investigate criminal activity and county government and issue reports to the public.* The grand jury, selected by the county's superior court judges, serves for a period of one year and acts as the county's "watchdog." At the end of that year, it must submit a final report to the

## Our Judicial System

## CORRECTION AND REHABILITATION
www.cdc.state.ca.us

California has over 161,000 prison convicts (about 2.1% of our population) and about 5,000 minors in the California Youth Authority system in an ever increasing population. Housing all the inmates in California costs over $5.2 billion a year and climbing. How will California deal with this problem?

Reformers argue there's a better and cheaper way. Hard-liners feel that the laws are not strict enough and want stiffer penalties for certain crimes.

The cost of keeping a prisoner in jail for a year is over $34,000. Hard-liners would argue that these same people would cost society more than that amount if they were left on the streets to continue their crimes.

**Unionized state prison guards,** Davis' biggest campaign contributors, were given contracts which allowed increased sick days without a doctor's verification. As a result, productivity lost by sick time increased by 500,000 hours, while absences caused overtime costs to increase by 100,000 hours. Union guards may retire at age is 50 with 90% of their salary.

county board of supervisors. The grand jury has the power, in unusual cases, to indict someone. An **INDICTMENT** *is a complaint against a person, charging that person with a crime.*

# Chapter 8

## Chapter Summary

California's judicial system is primarily a state (but does include federal) entity. It is a network of courts, agencies, and other groups including police departments, the state bar, and the prison and parole systems.

The California court system has three levels.

Superior Courts primarily function as "trial" courts, handling civil cases and divorce proceedings, guardianship petitions, probates, and some serious criminal and juvenile offenses.

Small Claims Courts are a type of lower court specializing in simple civil cases where the judgment amount is currently $5,000 or less.

Generally appeals of disputed cases from lower or trial courts rise to the next level, the Court of Appeal. These appellate courts re-examine cases based upon legal error, not factual correctness. There are six District Courts of Appeal in California helping to relieve the case load of the California Supreme Court.

The Supreme Court is the highest court in the state. Its decisions are binding over all other courts. The Supreme Court hears lower court appeals or may take a case directly from a lower court if it is felt to have constitutional significance. The court consists of a Chief Justice and six Associate Justices, each serving twelve-year terms. They are appointed by the governor but must be approved by the electorate in the next gubernatorial election. All Supreme Court and Courts of Appeal appointments are reviewed and confirmed by a Commission on Judicial Appointments.

The U.S. Supreme Court will only hear a case from the state court if it involves federal constitutional issues. The federal court insures that state court rulings and laws passed by the state legislature conform to the U.S. Constitution.

Criminal cases are categorized as either infractions (minor crimes), misdemeanors (more serious crimes), or felonies (very serious crimes). Plea bargaining is an agreement between the prosecutor and defense attorney to accept a plea of guilty to a lesser crime. Such arrangements ease congestion in the courts, as the accused is convicted without the need of a trial.

Some convicted offenders are allowed to serve their prison sentences on probation.

# Our Judicial System

In a criminal case, the district attorney is the prosecuting attorney for the government at the county level. The plaintiff is the party filing a court action while the defendant is the person or entity being sued or charged with a crime. The defense attorney represents the defendant. In a criminal case, this will often be a public defender when the defendant cannot afford an attorney.

After being arrested, an accused person is entitled to an arraignment before a judge where he or she is formally made aware of the charges and informed of his or her legal rights. At this point the individual may be held in custody, released on bail (as set by the judge), or released on his or her own recognizance.

In civil cases, the plaintiff files a case against the defendant, who is summoned to court and responds to the complaint. Both sides are heard (including discovery and presentation of evidence), and a decision, usually involving some payment of damages, is made.

Police officers are employed by a city to uphold justice. Sheriffs work for the county, often functioning as "the police" in unincorporated areas that have no police force. The Highway Patrol are state peace officers who protect our vast highway system. State Police protect state buildings and officials. A Marshal is a county peace officer serving our court system, guarding courtrooms, serving court papers, and evicting tenants if ordered by the court.

Citizens participate directly in the justice system by serving as witnesses and on juries. In civil and criminal trials this consists of up to twelve men and women charged with rendering a verdict. A Grand Jury consists of 19 citizens (23 in Los Angeles). It investigates crimes and government operations and issues a final report to the county board of supervisors.

## Class Discussion Questions

1. Does the governor appoint all judges?

2. How can the general public remove an unwanted judge?

3. What are the most serious types of crimes?

4. In your opinion, what types of investigations should your grand jury undertake?

5. Can you name at least four types of peace officers?

# Chapter 9
# *Cities and Counties at the Crossroads*

www.csac.counties.org (counties)
www.searchgov.com (directory)

California's local governments are at a crossroads; they are suffering from neglect and a lack of political power at the local level. Our cities and counties are designed so that there are no powerful executive leaders; they have no administrative power close to that possessed by the governor of the state or the president of the United States. The mayors have little power to run their cities and power at the county level is too diversified. Let's examine the situation.

Our local governments, which include counties, cities, districts and regions, affect each of us directly on a daily basis. The purpose of this chapter is to familiarize you with: (1) What local government services are available and how they affect all of us; (2) What functions are performed by each segment of our local governments and how to identify them; (3) How each local government unit taxes and what it spends on its operating budget; (4) An overview of how effectively each government unit is performing.

How our local governments are performing:

**COUNTIES**............................................ are just surviving
**CITIES**................................................ are just getting by
**SCHOOL DISTRICTS**................ show signs of improvement
**OTHER DISTRICTS**.................................... are doing well
**REGIONS**................... may be the solution to local problems

Chapter 9

# Counties

www.co.sacramento.ca.us

## TYPES OF COUNTIES

*COUNTIES* are large geographic areas initially established to bridge the gap between city governments and the state by providing services. Counties are political subdivisions of the state and their powers, duties, and obligations are set by the state legislature. The county oversees many important services, such as providing health and welfare services, police and fire departments, courts, roads, and park services.

The first California Constitution in 1849 provided for the creation of 27 counties and for the election of a board of supervisors in each county. In the early years, the county was simply an extension of the legislature and was under its direct control. The Constitutional Revision of 1879 made the functions of counties similar throughout the state, thereby bringing into existence what are known as general law counties. *GENERAL LAW COUNTIES are counties that may establish the number of county officials and their duties, but must have the approval of the state legislature.*

In 1911 the state legislature adopted the Home Rule Amendment which allowed for the creation of charter counties. A *CHARTER (HOME RULE) COUNTY has its own charter (constitution) that allows more flexibility in collecting revenue-producing taxes, electing and appointing officials, and, in general, running and controlling the programs of the county.* *HOME RULE (local control) is the concept that local people are more familiar with, and therefore can solve, their problems better than some distant government body.*

## COUNTY BOARD OF SUPERVISORS

The *COUNTY BOARD OF SUPERVISORS is the county elected governing body, required by the legislature, that sets policy and budgets funds.* Most boards consist of five members (San Francisco has eleven) who are elected in nonpartisan elections for staggered, four-year terms.

## COUNTY REVENUES

*COUNTY REVENUE is the money that the county receives from all sources.* In Los Angeles county, for example, the estimated revenue sources, from July 1, 1999, to June 30, 2000, (best available details) were approximately:

## Cities and Counties at the Crossroads

**STATE ASSISTANCE (28%)**
**FEDERAL ASSISTANCE (19%)**
**PROPERTY TAXES (21%)**
**SALES TAXES AND OTHER FEES (32%)**

State and federal governments contribute 47% toward the budgets of the counties but also require the counties to pay out large sums for the poor through health and welfare programs.

### PROPOSITION 13 (PROPERTY TAX LIMITATION)

The fate of our California counties was sealed in 1978 with the passage of Proposition 13 (the Jarvis-Gann Property Tax Initiative). This law set limits on the once major source of revenue for counties—property taxes.

*PROPOSITION 13 limits the amount of annual property taxes to a maximum of 1% of the March 1, 1975, market value or selling price of the property, whichever is higher, plus the cumulative increase of 2% each year thereafter.*

Before Proposition 13, if the county had a budget shortage, the county would simply increase the property tax rate and pass the costs on to the taxpayer. With real estate values soaring, citizens watched their tax bills soar. Angry homeowners overwhelmingly voted in support of Proposition 13.

As a result of Proposition 13, county governments saw a massive loss in revenue amounting to billions of dollars each year. Property taxes were reduced to one percent from as high as four percent. The state had to pour large amounts of money into the counties, cities, school districts, etc., just to cover some of the loss. Thus, a great deal of the policy-making function shifted to the legislature in Sacramento.

### OTHER COUNTY OFFICIALS

1. Chief Administrative Officer
2. District Attorney and Public Defender
3. Assessor and Treasurer
4. Sheriff

**Chapter 9**

## THE NUMBER OF COUNTIES HAS GROWN TO 58

 www.co.sacramento.ca.us/links3.html

The original boundaries of the 27 counties have been split and redrawn over the years to the present 58 counties. The counties in California vary widely in size, political makeup, and geography.

## FUNCTIONS OF THE COUNTY

Whether under the laws of the state in general law counties, or the guidelines of the charter in home rule counties, each county has certain duties and responsibilities that must be performed. Many of these functions are delegated to the board of supervisors, who are responsible for their implementation and continuous supervision. Some of the more important county functions are:

1. **Education** – County Superintendent of Schools is responsible for the overall administration and distribution of funds to schools (K-12 and community college).
2. **Law enforcement and protection of property** – the County Sheriff is responsible for the areas in the county outside of larger cities, which generally have their own police departments.
3. **Local Agency Formation Commission (LAFCO)** – a county board of supervisor's-created body whose function is to determine the boundaries of any proposed incorporated city within that county's area.
4. **Bridges and highways** – It is a county's responsibility to maintain the roads that lead into the main highways.
5. **Recreation** – each county maintains county parks.
6. **General government** – The county budget gets its share from the collection of property taxes by the County Tax Collector, and a portion of the sales tax.

## COUNTIES LACK EXECUTIVE MANAGEMENT

One of the biggest shortcomings of county government is the inability of the public to hold one individual accountable for the condition of county government. Each county has at least five supervisors acting as its governing body, making it impossible to single out any individual as being responsible for action or inaction. The state may have a twelve person plural executive, but the responsibility rests with the governor. Some counties have experimented with a chief administrative officer, appointed by the

*Cities and Counties at the Crossroads*

## Hispanic Presence on the L.A. County Board of Supervisors

The **REDISTRICTING LAWSUIT** judgment redesigned district boundaries so Latino voting power was not diluted. Supervisor Gloria Molina of the newly created 1st District is the first Hispanic member to serve in over 115 years. Her presence, plus another newly elected member, will greatly change the make-up of the five-member Los Angeles County Board of Supervisors, which has traditionally been dominated by white conservatives.

board of supervisors to carry out its programs. Even with this position, most citizens are still lost when it comes to understanding who is responsible for county government.

## COUNTY EXPENDITURES

*COUNTY EXPENDITURES are the monies that are spent by a county to operate.* The money is disbursed in the form of a budget. The typical budget that the board of supervisors in each county is responsible for is broken down as follows (Ventura County example):

| | |
|---|---|
| **Public Protection** | 37% |
| **Health and Sanitation** | 22% |
| **Public Assistance** | 14% |
| **General Government Offices** | 16% |
| **Public Ways and Facilities** | 7% |
| **Education** | 1% |
| **Recreation** | 1% |
| **Debt Service** | 1% |
| **Reserves** | <u>1%</u> |
| | 100% |

Note that public protection (law enforcement), healthcare, public assistance, governemnt offices, and roads and facilities account for almost the entire county budget, leaving little available for other needed services.

### Chapter 9

# Cities

### A CITY IS CREATED BY INCORPORATING

In 1883, the California State Legislature adopted the Municipal Corporations Act, which classified cities according to population, and laid the groundwork for future incorporation of cities. *INCORPORATION is the process of legally forming a municipal corporation.* When referring to an incorporated area, one is talking about a city. An *UNINCORPORATED AREA is a part of a county that is not a city.*

To incorporate, a community must petition the County Board of Supervisors. The Local Agency Formation Commission (LAFCO) then holds hearings at which time the boundaries of the proposed city are set. A *LOCAL AGENCY FORMATION COMMISSION is the group that defines the exact boundary lines of cities and counties.* After approval by the LAFCO, an election is then called.

Before Proposition 13, homeowners in cities found themselves taxed twice by paying property taxes to both the county and city. Since the passage of Proposition 13, the city property tax is subtracted from the county property tax. Because of this, there is no longer any reason, for most areas, not to incorporate.

### GENERAL LAW CITIES

All newly incorporated cities must begin their existence as general law cities. *In a GENERAL LAW CITY, government functions are administered by a five-member city council, elected for four-year terms.* A city clerk and treasurer are also elected for four-year terms. Other officials are appointed by the council. The mayor is chosen from the council. Some cities have a city manager or chief administrator appointed by the city council to carry out its programs. This person holds office only as long as the council desires.

### CHARTER (HOME RULE) CITIES

After a city becomes a general law city, it may frame a charter of its own, much like a county, and become a charter city. *A CHARTER CITY frames its own charter, enabling its citizens to better deal with current problems.* Most cities with populations over 100,000 in California are charter cities.

The main advantage of a charter city is its increased power with regard to local control and government function. A charter city can exceed the tax rate that is imposed on general law cities. It can perform any municipal functions that do not violate state or national laws. Most importantly, it allows the people of the city to adjust their government to meet any special needs.

## MAYOR-COUNCIL VS. COUNCIL-MANAGER

In a mayor-council type of city government, a *MAYOR is the chief executive officer of the city*, and the *CITY COUNCIL is usually a five to fifteen member nonpartisan board that is elected to handle the executive business of the city*. A *STRONG MAYOR SYSTEM usually allows the mayor some veto power over the council and power to appoint and remove certain city officials*. The best example of a strong mayor system in California is the city of San Francisco. A *WEAK MAYOR SYSTEM is one in which the office of mayor is more of a ceremonial position, with the mayor being selected from among the city council members*.

In a *COUNCIL-MANAGER form of city government, the people elect a city council and a mayor*. This is the most popular form of city government in California. The duties of the mayor are mostly ceremonial in nature. The council appoints a city manager to conduct the business of the city. A *CITY MANAGER is a professional manager who implements the city council's programs*. Over the years, the shift has been from an engineering background for a city manager toward a business background.

## OTHER CITY ADMINISTRATORS

1. City attorneys (prosecutors/public defenders)
2. City clerk
3. Police chief
4. Fire chief
5. Fiscal officials
6. Planning and community development officials
7. Public works officials
8. Recreation, parks, and community services officials
9. Librarians

## HOW CITIES ACQUIRE AND SPEND THEIR MONEY

A city acquires most of its funds from fees and activities that occur or are generated within the city. The following is an example of sources for San Diego's general fund revenues for the 2004 fiscal year:

**City Revenue**

| | |
|---|---|
| Property Tax | 26.9% |
| Sales Tax | 16.8% |

**Chapter 9**

| | |
|---|---|
| Money and Property Fees | 11.1% |
| Motor Vehicle License Fees | 10.1% |
| Current Services | 9.6% |
| Transient Occupancy | 7.8% |
| Transfers from Other Funds | 5.9% |
| Fines, Forfitures, and Penalties | 3.7% |
| Licenses and Permits | 3.3% |
| Others | 4.8% |

## COUNTIES BILL CITIES FOR SERVICES

Proposition 13 fixed property tax rates at 1% of the purchase price. The state legislature's power over the counties was increased because the amount of property taxes distributed back to the counties decreased. (Reallocation of property taxes by the state is given as follows: schools - 55%; county - 18%; districts - 18.4%; cities - 8.6%.)

As a result, counties rely more upon an increased distribution from sales taxes for their funding. The counties now have an incentive to increase sources of sales taxes by, among other things, permitting more strip, auto, and regional malls, or "Big Box Stores," like Wal-Mart.

Since commercial properties bring in sales taxes, which residential properties do not, there is no incentive given to counties and cities to permit zoning for affordable residential housing for the middle class and poor.

The state legislature allowed our under-funded counties to charge the cities within their county a "prisoner booking fee" and "property tax collection fee." This greatly concerns our California cities because they see this as the first in a series of steps that could mandate programs in the county for which the cities would be charged.

The city government provides the following services:

1. **Protective services** – Includes law enforcement, fire protection and civil defense. The highest percentage of funds is spent on these items.
2. **Recreation, health, education** – This includes parks and playgrounds. Health services are often in conjunction with county programs. Schools are run and maintained through school districts.
3. **Public works** – Improvement and maintenance of city streets, off-street parking, collection of trash and sanitation.
4. **General government** – Most cities utilize the county tax facilities to collect tax money.

# Districts

## DISTRICT FUNCTIONS

**DISTRICTS** *are geographic units designated for a specific governmental purpose, usually to provide a public service, such as mosquito abatement, flood control, and education.*

Districts can co-exist with a city or county but often they do not. There are about 6,000 districts in California, of which at least 1,000 are school districts.

## CREATION OF A DISTRICT

The establishment and organization of districts is provided for by state law. In order to form a district, a petition must be signed by the voters living within the boundaries of the proposed district. This petition is presented to the board of supervisors. A majority vote is needed by the board, or in some cases the electorate, to establish a district.

## SCHOOL DISTRICTS

The largest category of districts is the school districts. There are over 1,000 school districts in California. Every segment of California is divided into school districts. School districts include: elementary, high school, unified (K-12), union (high school district that encompasses several elementary districts), and community college.

Each school district has a board of education. The board of education generally consists of five members chosen in a nonpartisan election held within each district. The board has the responsibility of hiring principals, teachers, and all support staff for the district. It also adopts the school budget and determines the curriculum.

Each board is accountable to the state board of education, the ten member board appointed by the governor and administered by the state superintendent of public instruction. Each community college board of trustees has individual power to govern its own district. It is overseen by the state board of governors of the 108 community colleges, serving 2.9 million students.

www.cde.ca.gov **(Department of Education)**
www.mwd.dst.ca.us **(MWD)**

### Chapter 9

## WATER DISTRICTS

The Metropolitan Water District (MWD) was organized to provide Southern California with water to supplement its dwindling water supply.

Running along the Pacific Ocean from Oxnard to the Mexican border and inland for 70 miles, the MWD boundaries extend into six counties: San Diego, San Bernardino, Riverside, Orange, Los Angeles, and Ventura. The MWD supplies about half of the water used within its service area and is expected to handle nearly all of the anticipated increases in the future. Of course, the amount of water supplied will depend on deliveries from the California Aqueduct and the Colorado River Aqueduct.

# *Regional Governance*

## TREND FROM COUNTY TO REGIONAL DISTRICTS

The dramatic growth of Los Angeles, Ventura, Orange, Riverside, and San Bernardino counties has created a mostly urban area where the boundaries of counties and cities are so close together that they are hard to distinguish.

A **REGION** *is a large geographic unit that can include many cities and counties and cover a large portion of a state.* The common problems of cities and counties have led to the idea of regional governance.

**REGIONAL GOVERNANCE** *is the process of regional planning and policy making with the help of cities, counties, and businesses within the region.* Water shortages, air pollution, and transportation are just some of the issues which cross city or county lines and might be handled more efficiently at the regional level. When counties or cities are overwhelmed by a problem and underwhelmed by the resources needed to handle it, a regional approach seems to be the best answer.

Regional financing is the new way to solve regional problems. Los Angeles county is now collecting an additional half-cent sales tax to help solve transportation problems by linking together transit lines from many cities within the county. The Metropolitan Water District helps furnish most of the water for Southern California and bills according to usage. This trend will continue with regard to our air quality and waste management.

## COUNCILS OF GOVERNMENT

A **COUNCIL OF GOVERNMENT (COGs)** *is an association of city and county government officials, within a given region, whose purpose is to find solutions to*

> ### Hydrogen Fuel Cell Vehicles
>
> An exciting alternative to the gas-powered internal combustion engine may be the fuel cell-powered vehicle. A hydrogen fuel cell acts like a battery, converting hydrogen and oxygen into water and producing electricity to power an automobile engine. Most major automakers and private industry companies are investing millions in fuel cell engines. Today, the cost is prohibitive for the average car buyer, but technology and innovation may possibly change that. These vehicles offer the promise of a pollution-free mode of transportation. Hydrogen-powered buses are already in use at Georgetown University, Vancover in British Columbia, and in Palm Springs, California. In addition, the federal government has fostered this technology by making research and development funds available.

*common problems.* These COGs help solve common area problems quickly and cooperatively while maintaining the home rule style of government.

The Southern California Association of Government (SCAG) **(www.scag.ca.gov)** and the Association of Bay Area Governments (ABAG) **(www. abag.ca.gov)** are California's two major COGs.

ABAG has been successful in making regional plans for such important matters as transportation, refuse disposal, recreational facilities, and shoreline development. The SCAG is the largest COG in the United States, serving over 13 million people in a 38,000 square mile area. SCAG has been successful in coordinating the planned connection between the Southern California Rapid Transit District (SCRTD) and the Orange County Transit District (OCTD).

Most of California's regional problems are not being financed or solved by the federal or state government. Clean air and pollution standards by the Air Quality Management District (AQMD) have been made strict to reduce air pollution for the region. Federal standards, although well meaning, do not take into account Southern California's unique air pollution problems. So basically the federal government has complicated matters rather than offered viable solutions. Frankly, the state and federal governments have given Southern California mandates regarding air pollution but have not given the area the funds with which to accomplish these mandates. *MANDATES are the requirements for programs implemented by the state or federal government.*

Chapter 9

# Chapter Summary

Our California city and county governments face great challenges for the future. Greater demands are being placed on them than ever before, but local government lacks the definitive political clout necessary to effectively administer these services.

Counties are large geographical areas that bridge the gap between cities and the state by providing services at the local level. The California Constitution created the original 27 counties. There are now 58. The original counties were considered general law counties, and functioned only under the close supervision of the state legislature. Later, under the Home Rule Amendment of 1911, counties were permitted to designate themselves as charter (or home rule) counties permitting more autonomy to set policy and collect taxes.

A county government is administered by the County Board of Supervisors, usually five members elected to four-year terms. They decide public policy, budget funds, and make various local appointments. County governments are primarily responsible for several important public functions: education, law enforcement, Local Agency Formation Commission (LAFCO), maintenance of bridges and highways, recreation, and taxes.

County revenue also comes from the state (28%), the federal government (19%), property taxes (21%), sales taxes, and other fees (32%). These state and federal contributions are not without strings attached, and most of the money they give the counties is passed on directly to the public as health and welfare programs.

In 1978, Proposition 13 passed, limiting the amount of property taxes that could be collected by the county. Local governments saw a loss in revenue and the state had to fill the void, pouring millions of dollars into the counties to keep their schools, law enforcement, recreation, and other necessary programs operating. But with each dollar came more state control.

Counties spend most of their budgets (Ventura County example) on public protection (37%), health and sanitation (22%), as well as public assistance (14%), general government offices (16%), and public ways and facilities (7%). Very little is left for other areas such as education (1%), recreation (1%), debt service (1%), and reserves (1%).

# Cities and Counties at the Crossroads

Cities are created by incorporating, a process that is similar to forming a business corporation. They are formed from unincorporated areas of the county or split from other cities with the proper voters' approval. All cities start as general law cities but most become charter (home rule) city when its population grows and it wants less state regulation.

In a council-manager form of city government, which is the most common in California, the city is run by a professional city manager.

In the mayor-council form of city government, the mayor and council direct the different agencies that run the city. These cities are governed by a nonpartisan elected board of 5 to 15 members called a city council and a mayor who is selected to lead this group. Either the mayor is elected by the city council or is elected separately by the voters. If the mayor comes from a weak mayor system, the duties are mostly ceremonial. In a strong mayor system, the mayor can make appointments and remove certain city officials.

Although cities vary greatly, most cities collect their money from these sources: sales taxes and hotel taxes, real property taxes, cigarette taxes, development, and other fees. Cities spend their money mostly on: 1) police and fire protection; 2) health, recreation, and education; 3) public works, off-street parking, and sanitation; and 4) city personnel and elections.

There are about 6,000 districts in California. Districts are geographical units designed for a specific governmental purpose, such as flood control, mosquito abatement, or for schools. Perhaps one of the best known districts is the Metropolitan Water District (MWD). There are more than 1,000 school districts (K-12 and 108 community colleges). Regional governance may take the place of a local government on certain issues in the future because many of California's problems cross over city and county lines.

Chapter 9

## Class Discussion Questions

1. What made the formation of California cities so popular?

2. What are the effects on the state caused by diverse cultural and ethnic backgrounds?

3. What are the differences between California cities using either a weak or strong mayoral system?

4. What are the pros and cons of amending Proposition 13?

5. What are the strong and weak points of (county, city, district, and regional) governmental units in California?

# Cities and Counties at the Crossroads

# Chapter 10
# Our State Budget Crisis

## CALIFORNIA'S STATE BUDGET CRISIS

 www.dof.ca.gov

The California state budget crisis is directly related to our increasing population growth. Our budget is currently showing a deficit, business taxes are at an all time high, and our population is growing so fast that the state's resources cannot possibly keep up with the added demands. California's schools and jails are overcrowded, highways are congested, more landfills are closing, and more people than ever are on county health care. The system cannot keep up.

Remember, it is estimated that California's population will increase by about 5.5 million between 2000 and the year 2010. This amounts to a 17% increase, from 33.9 million to 39.7 million. No matter how one looks at our state's growth pattern, it is constantly growing larger.

Some say that all we need to continue our road to recovery is maintain our high level of taxation and create new laws. This is not a realistic position to take. Our taxes are very high and if they are increased even more, businesses will leave the state, taking needed jobs with them. Californians are already among the highest taxed people in the United States. The solution is to operate our state government more like a business. With some good leadership from state and local politicians, the problems facing California can be addressed. The state has run out of simple answers, higher taxes. What is left are hard political choices about where to cut spending to get the most out of budget dollars.

**Chapter 10**

## *California's Population is Growing Younger*

California's population is growing younger. Our retired population is shrinking while the number of children is growing at an unprecedented rate. The working group in the middle that pays most of the taxes is declining. To illustrate this point, California can be divided into three groups:

1. **EARNERS** (Age 18 to 64 – Working population)
2. **SPENDERS** (65 and older – Social security and pensioners)
3. **USERS** (Mostly under 18 – Receive public services: education, child care, welfare, and public healthcare)

**"Earners"** are declining in percentage terms. Parents of the baby boomers have retired and soon the baby boomers themselves will start leaving the work force.

**"Spenders"** are retirees living on social security who are positive contributors to the economy because they spend money and pay more than their fair share in state sales taxes. Unfortunately, over one million seniors have left the state in the last decade.

The **"users"** group are younger and use California's public service tax dollars in the form of education, child care, welfare, and public healthcare. The huge growth within this group is largely due to higher birthrates among an increasing immigrant population.

The end result of these demographic changes is that they drive up state and local government spending, while at the same time reducing the revenue generated by state income taxes and sales taxes.

*Our State Budget Crisis*

## RECOVERY (AFTER THE 2003 BUDGET CRISIS AND ECONOMIC SLOWDOWN)

The amount of state income taxes collected after the recall will continue to increase as the economy recovers from the slowdown. Remember: the days of easy answers are over for California—only hard choices remain about our future.

# The California State Budget

The *STATE BUDGET is the state government's financial plan for spending and taxing that is proposed by the governor and passed by the legislature for each fiscal year.*

Federal, state, and county governments use a fiscal year instead of a calendar year. The *GOVERNMENTAL FISCAL YEAR is a 365-day year that starts on July 1 and ends on June 30.* For example, if the governor, mayor, or a school board member refers to the 2004-2005 fiscal year, he or she is referring to the year from July 1, 2004 to June 30, 2005.

There are no deficits allowed in state budgets. A *DEFICIT occurs when the current money collected from the people, in the form of taxes, is not enough to pay for the agreed-upon expenses.*

## THE BUDGET PROCESS

The complicated budget process covers an 18-month period. The budget phases, lasting six months each, are:

1. Budget construction stage: "What do you want."
2. Department of Finance refinement stage: "Be realistic."
3. Legislative debate stage: "Only getting what we give."

Each January, after the governor's State of the State Address, the budget is submitted to the legislature. The legislature, after debating it at length and passing it with the required two-thirds vote of both houses, submits the approved budget to the governor. The submission date to the governor is June 15, but the legislature often drags it on.

Remember: the governor has line item veto power. The *LINE ITEM VETO means the governor can eliminate or reduce any budget item he or she does not like.* The budget then goes back to the legislature, which has the constitutional power to override the governor's veto with a two-thirds vote in each house—they seldom succeed.

*Chapter 10*

## CALIFORNIA'S BUDGET PROBLEMS

California's demographics show the increasing number of children, people needing county health and welfare services, and the number of cars on the highways.

The budget crisis of 2003 and beyond has made us ask an all important question: How will California handle its growth problems in a state where the residents are already among the most taxed in the country? There are only difficult answers when seeking ways to reduce the budget. Reasonable solutions to our growth problems must be given priorities. The budget can then be tightened by searching for new practical answers. The budget problems created by our extensive population growth over the past decades are here. The question is how will we deal with all these problems at once?

### Proposition 98

The voters passed Proposition 98. It established minimum levels of spending for schools and community colleges at 40% of the annual budget from the general fund.

## *Types of State Taxes*

### THE FOUR MAIN TAXES

In order to understand California's basic tax structure, it is best to look at the four main sources of state taxes in detail. Who pays these taxes, and what rate they pay, are political questions. The state's taxing policy, which is implemented by our governor and legislature, constantly changes over time.

#### #1 – State Personal Income Taxes

> **FACT:** California is a "Trillion Dollar Economy." The amount of taxes will increase as will spending.

The ***STATE FRANCHISE TAX BOARD (www.ftb.ca.gov)*** *is the California state agency that collects state income taxes from individuals and corporations.* The state personal income tax is the single largest source of taxes in California. Currently the state income tax rate goes up to 9.3% for those in

## Our State Budget Crisis

### State Taxes 2003-2004
### Where State Taxes Come From:

| | | |
|---|---|---|
| #1 | Personal Income Taxes | 37.4% |
| #2 | State Sales Tax | 29.8% |
| #3 | Bank & Corporation Income Taxes | 9.1% |
| #4 | Motor Vehicle Fees | 8.4% |
| #5 | Highway Users Taxes | 4.6% |
| #6 | Insurance Tax | 1.8% |
| #7 | Tobacco Tax | 1.0% |
| #8 | Estate Tax | 1.0% |
| #9 | Miscellaneous Minor Taxes | 6.9% |

the highest bracket. But remember, federal income taxes, which have a top rate of 39.6%, must be paid in addition to the state income taxes. Some other states, such as Nevada, Florida, and Washington, do not even charge their citizens any personal income tax. This is another reason why some of our more affluent residents are tempted to leave California.

State income taxes are indexed. *INDEXING is the periodic adjustment of income tax brackets to eliminate the effects of inflation.* This means that if the inflation rate is 3% for the year, the tax bracket will also go up by 3% to compensate for the difference. The taxpayer, although making more money, may still remain in the same tax bracket.

#2 – State Sales Taxes

The *STATE BOARD OF EQUALIZATION (www.boe.ca.gov) is the California state agency that collects state sales taxes from businesses which, in turn, collect taxes from the consumer at the point of purchase.* Wholesalers do not pay sales taxes because they are not the ultimate consumer. The current sales tax rate is 7.5%, but this base rate can be increased on an individual county basis, if approved by the voters, by up to three-quarters of a percent (.75%) for transportation or other uses. In L.A. county, for example, the sales tax is 8.25%.

#3 – Bank and Corporation Income Taxes

In addition to collecting income taxes on individuals, the state also collects income taxes on corporations, whose shares of stock are mostly owned by individuals, and the pension plans of most unions or businesses. If we add

**Chapter 10**

personal income taxes (37.4%) and corporation income taxes (9.1%), it means California receives 46.5% of its revenue from income taxes.

**#4 – Motor Vehicle Fees**

Motor vehicle fees are a fact of life for California, the state with the most cars. But the recall doomed the 300% increase in the 2003 Davis Budget that brought so much force behind the recall election.

## EFFECTS OF TAXES: (THE POOR AND THE WEALTHY)

Taxes do not affect all people in the same way. Certain taxes affect the poor more than the wealthy, and certain taxes hardly affect the poor but definitely hurt the wealthy. The goal should be a tax policy that requires very little from the poor and more (but not too much) from the wealthy. Of course, the same policy would collect most of the taxes from the middle group referred to as "average" Californians.

A *REGRESSIVE TAX is a tax that is larger, as a percentage of income, for lower income people*. A good example of a regressive tax is the California state sales tax. This tax takes up a larger portion of the lower income individual's personal budget because almost all of his or her income is used to buy items subject to this tax. It has a big impact on people who have the least amount of money. If the same tax rate is paid by all, it is regressive.

A *PROGRESSIVE TAX is a tax that increases percentage-wise as the wealth of the taxpayer increases*. The best example of a progressive tax is the California state income tax on individuals and businesses. Poor people may not pay any income taxes, middle income Californians pay a large amount, and the wealthy pay the most, on an individual basis. This tax affects the rich the most because they are in the highest tax bracket and therefore pay the most money.

*SIN TAXES are the taxes paid for the purchase and consumption of alcoholic beverages and tobacco products*. These taxes have increased dramatically in recent years. The tax is not only applied to hard liquors but also to wines and beers.

## TAXES WILL REMAIN HIGH

California's taxes will remain high in the foreseeable future because of the many problems created by our continuous population growth. Most of the badly needed solutions will require funds that the state does not possess

# Our State Budget Crisis

at this time. So the challenge to the political leadership is: How will it decide, among competing alternatives, which programs will receive the most money and attention?

## Spending: Where Taxes Go

### THE FOUR LARGEST EXPENDITURES

The four largest expenditures represent 88% of the state's budget. In descending order of cost, they are: #1 Schools and Community Colleges; #2 Health and Welfare; #3 Higher Education; and #4 Prisons and the Youth Authority. California's economic recovery will someday provide more money in the budget for newer, more innovative programs after funding these big costly programs.

**#1 COST – Education: K-12 and Community Colleges**

More money is spent educating our students from kindergarten through high school and supporting community college students than on any other state function. Education represents 41.5% of the state budget. Each school or college district is technically owned by the state but governed, controlled, and administered by a local board that is elected by the voters. *LOCAL CONTROL means that the administrators and teachers are hired by the local board of education to administer and teach the subjects approved by the board.*

The state provides 85% of all the educational costs to each district. About 12% of the money for schools and community colleges comes from the local governments that collect funds in the form of real estate property taxes. In addition, the state lottery generates about 3% of the funds.

It costs approximately $6,624 a year, per student, to educate a child in the K-12 public school system. Further, most community college students do not realize that it costs over $3,400 annually to educate a full-time student. Even though community colleges charge students about $540 ($18 a unit) a year for tuition and fees, they are still getting one of the best educational bargains anywhere in the United States.

**#2 COST – Health and Welfare**

**Health Services:** Public health care has been constantly declining because of the relentless population increases. Providing health services to Californians who do not have health insurance is nearly impossible under the current system. The number of people who want free health care keeps

Chapter 10

## State Spending 2003-2004
### Spending of Tax Money:

| | | |
|---|---|---|
| #1 | Education (K-12, Community Colleges) | 41.2% |
| #2 | Health and Welfare | 32.9% |
| #3 | Higher Education | 12.2% |
| #4 | Prisons, Youth Authority | 7.9% |
| #5 | Courts/Legislature/General Government | 2.1% |
| #6 | Natural Resources | 1.2% |
| #7 | Tax Relief (Homeowners & Seniors) | 1.0% |
| #8 | Business, Transportation, & Housing | 0.7% |
| #9 | State and Consumer Services | 0.6% |
| #10 | Environmental Protection Agency | 0.2% |

rising. The cost of all health care is increasing at such a fast pace that even a good state health program cannot keep up under current legislation.

**Welfare:** California has 12.3% of the U.S. population, but must support 16% of the nation's health and welfare recipients. Unfortunately, each year health and welfare continues to take up a larger and larger portion of the state budget.

### #3 COST – Higher Education

A recent increase of 30% has forced students on University of California campuses to pay more for tuition. Student fees at the California State University are expected to stabilize, meaning higher education in California will continue to be a bargain.

The 2003-2004 annual undergradute fees are as follows:

1. **University of California** – California resident - $4,271; nonresident - $13,730.

2. **California State University** – California resident - $2,566; nonresident - also pay tuition of $188 per quarter or $288 per semester.

www.cccco.edu (California Community Colleges)
www.calstate.edu (California State University)
www.ucop.edu (University of California)

# Our State Budget Crisis

## Budget Crisis

### $38 Billion Deficit (2003-2004)
### $8-12 Billion Deficit (2004-2005)

State governments are, by law, not allowed to have deficits. A **DEFICIT** *is when a government agency spends more money than it acquires in tax revenue.* Only the federal government is allowed to run a deficit; and then the only time it would be appropriate is when the economy is in a downturn and the deficit is needed to stimulate job growth. The federal government has the central bank, known as the Federal Reserve Board, to manipulate the federal debt (created by deficit) to increase growth, stabilize inflation, and keep unemployment in check, ultimately for the prosperity of the entire nation.

### Recall for Fiscal Mismanagement

Huge continuing state deficits, caused by the former governor and the legislature's overspending, were the economic catalyst behind the governor's recall. Davis' reaction to the controversial "energy crisis" resulted in huge increases in electricity rates, and a big bite out of the already dwindling state budget. This, combined with other bad financial decisions, brought about Governor Davis' downfall and subsequent recall.

#### #4 COST – Prisons, Youth Authority

There are over 161,000 men and women in California prisons, more than any other state. The public's fear of crime, which is fed by the news media, demands that politicians be tough on criminals. The problem is that it costs over $34,000 a year to house a prisoner. In many respects, it would benefit us to come up with alternatives to prisons for non-violent offenses, such as individual abuse of drugs or alcohol. If the state could reduce the annual $4.3 billion budget by one billion, just think of the possibilities. Sadly, 70% of released prisoners are returned to prison within three years.

## MOST SPENDING IS EARMARKED

Most state government spending is earmarked for special purposes. **EARMARKED FUNDS** *are those that have been committed and budgeted ahead of time to accomplish a certain purpose.* An example of earmarked funds are

**Chapter 10**

gas taxes, which are used to build highways, even though the state now needs more funds for mass transit systems. Regardless of increasing public needs, our government is handcuffed, it can't spend earmarked funds.

## Bonds Mean Debt

When the state of California needs to borrow money, the amount is too large to be borrowed from a lending institution. The state must sell bonds to the general public in order to raise funds. A *BOND is a debt, a loan in increments of $1,000, made to the state of California, which will be repaid by the state to the owner of the bond on a certain date, usually in 20 years*. In effect, this is an installment credit program to purchase buildings or finance construction projects. Voters must approve each bond issue. There are two types of bonds.

A *GENERAL OBLIGATION BOND is secured by everything the state owns*. It is used when the project the bond is funding will not earn money.

A *REVENUE BOND is backed up only by the revenue generated by that project or taxing district*. The state uses revenue bonds to finance dams, canals, bridges, and other projects that can generate income. Buyers of these bonds rely on credit rating agencies to analyze the credit worthiness of the issue.

## Business Climate

California may lead the nation in creating new corporations, but when operating expenses get too high, they move to a state where income taxes are lower.

A healthy business climate creates and keeps jobs. Until recently, California citizens never thought businesses would leave the state. Former Governor Davis supported organized labor legislation, raising the cost of wages. One example being that overtime is now paid after 8 hours per day, versus most other states that define overtime as anything over forty hours a week. This costs California businesses over $1,000,000,000 a year!

The last three years of the Davis Administration saw job losses of 223,900, but government jobs rose (bigger government) 121,700, so the private job sector loss was really 345,600.

## Our State Budget Crisis

## California's Bond Rating Became Worst in the Nation – "BBB"

Standard & Poor's, one of the leading Wall Street credit rating firms, lowered California's rating to a worst-in-the-nation "BBB," a move that will cost the state $38 million and perhaps $1 billion in future higher interest costs.

The rating is just two notches above dreaded junk-bond status, the point at which many big institutional investors can't buy the bonds. Standard & Poor's punished California for its overspending by lowering the state's bond rating a jaw-dropping three levels. Usually, credit ratings drop a single step at a time. Moody's Investor Service, the other big credit rating firm, has threatened to further downgrade California's ratings.

**California now has a credit rating of "BBB," only two levels above junk bond status.**

The lowered bond rating means that California will pay more in interest in order to attract investors. If California's ratings are further reduced, many large investors will be unable to purchase or hold the bonds because of investment restrictions, regardless of the higher interest rates that are offered.

**California received the worst bond rating in the nation and the worst in California's history.**

This rating matches the lowest that any state has ever received. California has not always had poor credit ratings. Before Governor Gray Davis, California had a "AAA" rating—the highest possible.

The poor performance of California's government affects more than interest rates. It indicates that the California economy is likely to continue to struggle for some time. The reason is the state's budget shortfall, related tax increases, and increased worker's compensation insurance costs. These items increase business uncertainty and curb hiring and spending.

The "Davis budget" is an agreement to continue to borrow more money, instead of balancing spending and revenue. Until this underlying issue is solved, bond lenders will view California with great concern.

**This was a disaster for the state's gigantic municipal bond market.**

*Chapter 10*

## WHAT BUSINESSES TO ATTRACT

California's economy has always grown by attracting new and emerging firms and industries. Remember, California's economic strengths are:

1. Pacific Rim trade.
2. Advanced bio- and high-technology.
3. Entertainment and tourism.
4. Professional services, engineering, design, finance, etc.
5. Diversified manufacturing.

California's economy depends on a highly creative, technologically advanced and educated workforce, resulting in higher wages, which are necessary to afford high cost locations. We start and attract innovative companies that are on the cutting edge. These types of companies come here because of the state's strengths. These are the types of companies that we should encourage to do business in California.

California's continued growth depends on attracting the next generation of growth firms. We should be asking fast growing companies why they located here instead of asking firms why they are leaving. This focus on growth, always looking ahead, is the right direction for the state's economy.

# Our State Budget Crisis

# Chapter Summary

California's state budget is in a constant crisis. There is not enough money coming in to cover the basic cost of all the services that the state should provide to our citizens. This problem is growing worse due to relentless population growth. Every decade we add another six million people to drain already limited resources. Raising taxes is not the answer. Higher taxes only drive businesses away to other states or countries where they can operate less expensively. If businesses leave, so do jobs and tax money, damaging the economy even more. There are no simple answers, the future of California will depend on careful planning and intelligent leadership.

Much of the economic problem is the result of the population distribution between three economic groups: "earners," "spenders," and "users." "Earners" are the working population, ages 18 to 64. The older group, or "spenders," are retirees living on social security. Even though they are not still active in the workplace, they are good for the economy because they spend money and pay more than their fair share in state sales taxes. The biggest economic drain on the state is the "users" group, made up of children.

The state budget is the government's plan for spending and taxing for the next fiscal year. The fiscal year begins July 1 and ends June 30. A deficit occurs when the tax money collected is not enough to cover the legislatively agreed upon expenses. California, by law, must have a balanced budget—no deficit.

Money collected from the California personal income tax is the state's primary source of revenue. People in the highest brackets pay 9.3% of their income to the State Franchise Tax Board. The number two source of revenue is the state sales tax, collected by the State Board of Equalization. The current state sales tax rate base is 7.5%, although many counties add their own voter-approved sales tax on top of this for local uses. Our third largest taxing source is the income tax collected from banks and corporations. The vehicle and licensing fees collected by the Department of Motor Vehicles are the fourth source.

The state sales tax is an example of a "regressive tax." The same rate of tax is paid by rich and poor alike, but the sales tax hits poor people harder because they spend most of their money on items subject to this tax. A "progressive tax" is one that increases, as a percentage of income, as the wealth of the taxpayer increases. The state income tax is a good example. People with higher incomes are required to pay a higher tax rate.

**Chapter 10**

Education is the primary expenditure of the California state budget. The fiscal budget for K-12 and community colleges is 41.2% of the budget. Health and Welfare is the state's number two expense at 32.9%. Higher Education, the University of California and Cal State systems, has a cost of 12.2%. Prisons take up 7.9% of the budget.

When funds are committed in advance for a specific program, they are said to be "earmarked." Lottery money being used for public schools is a good example. The problem with earmarked funds is they deprive our government officials of discretion as priorities change.

When the state needs to borrow large amounts of money it issues "bonds." Bonds are a form of debt. The state borrows from the general public in increments of $1,000. These bonds are paid off later with interest. General obligation bonds are secured by all California assets, whereas revenue bonds are backed up only by the income from a particular project.

## Class Discussion Questions

1. What types of taxes generate the most income?

2. List the main expenditures of the state and calculate what percentage of the budget is available for new programs.

3. Is the state sales tax or the state income tax more regressive or progressive in nature?

4. Of what significance is the fact that the state's population is growing younger?

5. When voters approve bonds, who will pay them off?

# *Glossary*

**ABBREVIATIONS:** The following abbreviations are commonly used by the California Legislature:

**AB** – Assembly Bill
**SB** – Senate Bill
**ACA** – Assembly Constitutional Amendment
**SCA** – Senate Constitutional Amendment
**AJR** – Assembly Joint Resolution
**SJR** – Senate Joint Resolution
**ACR** – Assembly Concurrent Resolution
**SCR** – Senate Concurrent Resolution
**HR** – House Resolution (Assembly)
**SR** – Senate Resolution

**ABSENTEE BALLOT:** A ballot that is sent to the voter before the election, allowing that voter to mail-in or hand deliver his or her ballot if they know they can not make it to the polls on election day. The absentee ballot must be received back before the close of the polls.

**ACT:** A Bill passed by the Legislature.

**ADMISSION DAY:** September 9, 1850, the day that California became the 31st State admitted to the Union. Admission Day is celebrated each year on September 9.

**ADVISORY OPINION:** Issued by the California attorney general, it is a legal opinion of the legality or constitutionality of intended or finished courses of action.

**AMENDMENT:** An instrument for the changing in a law of in a state or federal constitution.

**ANNEXATION:** An action whereby one city gains legal jurisdiction over another nearby city or over an unincorporated area.

**APPELLATE COURT:** An appellate court hears appeals arising from the trial courts. In California, the Courts of Appeal and the California Supreme Court are generally considered appellate courts, but superior, municipal and justice courts can also be appellate courts.

**APPROPRIATION BILL:** A bill that authorizes funds to be spent from state revenues. **See:** Bill, Urgent Bill.

**APPORTIONMENT:** Division of the State into districts from which representatives are elected.

**ASSEMBLY:** The lower house of the California Legislature, whose 80 members are elected to two-year terms (three-term limit) from districts apportioned on the basis of population. **Compare:** Senate – Legislature, Speaker.

**ASSEMBLY RULES COMMITTEE:** A powerful committee that refers all bills to standing committees, as well as selecting and supervising the assembly support staff. The Speaker is the chairperson of the Rules Committee.

**ASSEMBLY SPEAKER PRO TEMPORE:** Elected by the members of the assembly to perform leadership duties during the speaker's absence or when the speaker is discussing compromises with his or her colleagues on the floor of the assembly. **Compare:** Speaker, President Pro Tempore.

**ASSESSMENT:** The valuation of property for the purpose of levying a tax or the amount of the tax levied.

**AT-LARGE ELECTIONS:** An election process whereby the entire population of a governmental area votes for each member of the city council, board of supervisors or other nonpartisan local government offices.

**ATTORNEY GENERAL:** California's independently elected director of the justice department, responsible for ensuring that the laws of the state are adequately and uniformly enforced. The second most important executive officer in the state after the governor.

**AUDITOR GENERAL:** Appointed by the joint legislative audit committee to assist the legislature by examining, auditing and reporting on the financial statements submitted by the executive branch.

**BEAR FLAG REVOLT:** A revolt by Americans in Mexican-ruled California that started on June 14, 1846, near Sonoma. It began because of fear that the Mexican government was about to move against American settlers. The original California Flag was created during this short-lived event.

**BICAMERAL:** A legislature is bicameral when it has two houses, or chambers. In California, the legislature is made up of the state senate, or "upper house," and the state assembly, or "lower house." A unicameral legislature is a one-house legislature.

**BILL:** A proposed law, introduced during a session, for consideration by the Legislature, and identified numerically in order of presentation; also, commonly, but incorrectly, refers to joint and Concurrent Resolutions and Constitutional Amendments. **See:** Appropriation Bill, Urgent Bill.

**BLANKET PRIMARY:** Voters can decide who they want for any office position on the ballot, no matter what political party the candidate is from.

**BLOCK GRANT:** A grant to be used for general purposes, given from one level of government to another. Of the 400 grants-in-aid given, only 14 are currently block grants. **See:** Grant-in-Aid, Categorical Grants.

**BOND:** A certificate of debt, issued by a government (or corporation), guaranteeing payment of the original investment, plus interest, by a specified future date. In California, bonds are debts in increments of $1000 that are usually paid off over a twenty year period. All bonds must be approved by the voters. **See:** General Obligation Bonds, Revenue Bonds.

**BUDGET (STATE):** A formal financial plan for a government (or other organization), listing proposed revenues and expenditures. In California, the budget is proposed, each fiscal year by the governor and then debated and passed by the legislature. **See:** Governmental Fiscal Year.

**CAL-SPAN:** Established in 1991 as a nonprofit company that distributes the television signal of the proceedings of the California Assembly to cable subscribers throughout the state.

**CALIFORNIA POLITICS:** Like all politics, it is the process of arriving at a consensus on how the state is to be governed.

**CAMPAIGN MESSAGE:** The theme of the person or the issue that the campaign will attempt to communicate to the voters. **See:** Campaign Strategy.

**CAMPAIGN STRATEGY:** A well thought-out tactical plan with winning an election as its goal, by identifying the audience, the message, the delivery and timing while considering the campaign resources. **See:** Campaign Message.

**CAPITAL PUNISHMENT OFFENSE:** A crime where the death penalty is prescribed by the court for the taking, or the involvement in the taking, of a human life.

**CAPITAL:** There are many meanings for this word: (a) It can refer to the land, buildings and any projects to be built on the land. (b) It refers to the death penalty or any crimes that may be punishable by death, hence the term "capital punishment." (c) It refers to the city that is the home of the governor and state legislature, in our case, Sacramento is the "capital" of California. (d) It can refers to the business use by a person or corporation to produce profits. Not to be confused with this spelling is "capitol," which is the building that houses the governor and the legislature.

**CATEGORICAL GRANTS:** Grants made for a specific purpose or to target a specific program. The restrictions of this type of grant leaves the recipient with very little discretion. **See:** Grant-in-Aid, Block Grant.

**CAUCUS:** An informal meeting of a group of the members of a political party. Also, the research staff and offices of the minority and majority leaders. Derived from an Algonquin Indian word.

**CHARTER CITIES:** Cities that have their own charter (constitution). When cities are created they are general law cities. They may later vote to change to a charter city. Most cities with populations over 100,000 are charter cities. **Compare:** General Law Cities.

**CHARTER COUNTIES:** Those counties that have their own constitutions, which allows for more flexibility in collecting revenue-producing taxes. **Compare:** General Law Counties.

**CHIEF CLERK:** An officer of the Assembly, elected by the members to direct the clerical staff and the preparation of daily printing and general publications, and to be of assistance to the presiding officer in interpreting the rules.

**CITY COUNCIL:** A five to fifteen member nonpartisan board that is elected at large or by districts, for four year terms, to handle the executive business of a city.

**CITY MANAGER:** An appointed executive given legal responsibility for the executive function of a local government. City managers are selected for their professional skills by the city council.

**CIVIL LAW (CASES):** Charges brought against private parties or organizations usually for business or financial reasons. **See:** Criminal Law (Cases).

**CIVIL SERVICE:** A system of government employment where positions are obtained through nonpolitical evaluations such as background characteristics and scores on tests and interviews. Employees in a civil service system are afforded protection from political interference.

**CLEMENCY:** The governor's power to reduce the sentence of a convicted felon for humanitarian purposes. **Compare:** Pardon, Reprieve.

**CLOSED PRIMARY:** A primary in which the voter can only receive a ballot of the party in which he or she is registered. California uses a closed primary system, with the exception of Independent Party voters, who can vote for the party of their choice. **See:** Blanket Primary.

**COALITION:** A temporary joining of groups of different views and political leanings that come together for the purpose of accomplishing something. For example, legislators from different parties join together to pass legislation that will benefit them all.

**COMMISSION ON JUDICIAL APPOINTMENTS:** Consists of three members who have the responsibility of confirming all judicial nominees to the California Courts of Appeal and Supreme Courts.

**COMMISSION ON JUDICIAL PERFORMANCE:** A commission of five judges, two attorneys and two private citizens that act as a monitor ("watchdog") of judges and their conduct in and out of the courtroom. Any disciplinary action is recommended to the California Supreme Court.

**COMMITTEE SYSTEM:** A system whereby the legislature is broken down into committees; a basic working component that can study all bills in depth. The main committees are the: 1) Standing Committees; 2) Joint Committees; 3) Fiscal Committees; 4) Conference Committees; 5) Select or Special Committees.

**COMMON CAUSE:** A nonpartisan citizens' group organized in 1969 to adopted by the Legislature or presented by initiative, requiring an affirmative vote of the electorate to become effective.

**CONSTITUTIONAL CONVENTION:** An accepted method to alter a state's (or national) constitution or to form an entirely new document that must then be submitted to the electorate for a ratification vote. Such a convention was held in California in 1879, resulting in our Second State Constitution.

**CONTRACT CITIES:** Cities that contract with the county to provide services desired by the city. Examples of such services are police protection, health services and street maintenance.

**CONTROLLER:** California's independently elected chief accountant and disbursement officer. The controller is the state's most important fiscal officer. **See:** Plural Executive.

**COUNCIL OF GOVERNMENT (COGS):** Regional planning agencies joined by cities and counties for the purpose of dealing with common area-wide problems. Examples include the Association of Bay Area Governments (ABAG) and the Southern California Association of Governments (SCAG).

**COUNSEL:** An attorney. **See:** legislative counsel.

**COUNTIES:** Established by the first California Constitution in 1849, counties originally numbered 27 and were basically operational arms of the Legislature. Today there are 57 counties and one "city and county" combination (San Francisco), each with a Board of Supervisors and delegated government functions such as education, law enforcement, property recording and assessment, judicial functions, tax collection and election administration. **See:** Charter County, General Law County. **Compare:** Cities, Special District, Board of Supervisors.

**COUNTY BOARD OF SUPERVISORS:** The legislative and administrative authority at the county level. Most counties elect five members to their boards for four-year staggered terms. San Francisco elects eleven members.

**COUNTY CENTRAL COMMITTEE:** The county political party group elected by popular vote from assembly districts. Additional members are party nominees from within the district. **See:** State Central Committee.

**COURTS OF APPEAL:** Set up to hear appeals from lower courts and to relieve the case load on the California Supreme Court. They only hear appeals based on legal, not factual, interpretation. There are six District Courts of Appeal located close to large population centers in California. **See:** Supreme Court.

**CRIMINAL LAW (CASES):** Criminal law deals with crimes, and determines what punishment (if any) is appropriate. **See:** Civil Law (Cases).

**CROSS-FILING:** A now prohibited practice in California in which a political candidate would run in both the the Democratic and Republican primaries and would not reveal his or her real true party affiliation. Utilizing this strategy, a candidate could be nominated by both major parties. Earl Warren (1943-1953) was the last governor to utilize cross-filing. Cross-filing was abolished in the 1950s.

**CROWD LOBBYING:** The practice of mobilizing large numbers of people to attend organizing rallies timed to influence a decision or specific legislation. **See:** Lobbyist.

**DAILY FILE:** A guide published daily that informs interested people of that day's business in both houses of the legislature.

**DAILY JOURNAL:** A guide published daily that informs interested people about what happened the preceding day in both houses of the legislature.

**DEFENDANT:** The person being sued (in a civil law case) or charged (in a criminal law case). **Compare:** Plaintiff.

**DEMOGRAPHIC INTEREST GROUP:** Populations that can be identified as a group of people that share characteristics such as income, age, and education. **See:** Interest Group.

**DEPARTMENT OF MOTOR VEHICLES (DMV):** The California state agency that issues drivers' licenses or photo identifications and handles the paperwork for vehicle licensing and registration.

**DIRECT DEMOCRACY:** The Initiative, referendum and recall are the citizens' tools for direct democracy. Average citizens can decide public issues directly through the use of these legislative tools and bypass their elected officials. **See:** Initiative, Referendum, Recall.

**DIRECT PRIMARY:** An early election for the purpose of selecting party candidates from among those nominated. It places the final responsibility of candidate selection with the voters, not the political party. **See:** Primary Election.

**DISTRICT (1):** That division of the State represented by a legislator, distinguished numerically, or by counties contained therein, determined on the basis of population. Not to be confused with special districts or school districts.

**DISTRICT (2):** Geographic units designed for a specific governmental purpose, usually to provide a public service, such as mosquito abatement, flood control and education. **See:** School District, Water District.

**DISTRICT ATTORNEY (D.A.):** The prosecuting attorney for the government at the county level.

**DROPOUT RATE:** The percentage of high school students that do not finish twelfth grade.

**EARMARKED FUNDS:** Funds that are designated, by law, for specific purposes. **See:** Revenue.

**EARNERS:** The segment of the population (Age 18 to 64) that is considered the "working population" of California. **See:** Spenders, Users.

**ECONOMICALLY DIVERSE:** Refers to the fact that any city, county or region has a wide-range of economic activities balanced so that no one industry dominates to the extent that, if eliminated, it would cause serious economic problems.

**ELECTORATE:** Refers to all persons qualified to vote, or only to those who actually voted in a particular election.

**EUREKA:** Refers to the gold rush in California and means "I have found it!" It also appears on the Great Seal of California.

**EX OFFICIO:** ("out of or because of one's office") The holding of a particular office by reason of holding another.

**EXPUNGE:** A motion by which action is deleted from the journal; i.e. "expunge the record."

**EXECUTIVE COMMITTEE:** A small group of high party officials who meet often to conduct party business in the party name. (p. 120) See: state central committee.

**EXPORTS:** Include any manufactured goods, agricultural produce, minerals and other items produced in the United States but purchased by other countries. **See:** Imports.

**FAIR POLITICAL PRACTICES COMMISSION:** A five member bipartisan state panel responsible for the administration and enforcement of the Political Reform Act. **See:** Political Reform Act.

**FELONY:** A serious offense against state law, such as armed robbery, drug trafficking and murder, involving a minimum penalty of one year in a state prison. **See:** Infraction, Misdemeanor.

**FISCAL YEAR (GOVERNMENTAL):** A 365 day year that starts on July 1 and ends on June 30.

**FULL FAITH AND CREDIT CLAUSE:** A provision that requires civil obligations (contract, etc.) that are enforceable in a civil proceeding in one state to be enforceable in any other state.

**GENERAL ELECTION:** The election held on the first Tuesday after the first Monday of November in even numbered years to elect nominees to such offices as president of the United States and governor of California.

**GENERAL LAW COUNTIES:** Those counties that, as needed, may establish the number of county officials and their duties but must have the approval of the state legislature. **Compare:** Charter County.

**GENERAL OBLIGATION BONDS:** A type of bond that is guaranteed by the full taxing power and good credit of the unit of government that issues it. **See:** Bond, Revenue Bonds.

**GENERAL SESSION (STATE LEGISLATURE):** A two-year period that starts at noon on the first Monday in December of even-numbered years and ends by November 30 of the following even-numbered year. **See:** Special Session.

**GERRYMANDER:** To divide into voting districts that give unfair advantage to one political party. Named after Elbridge Gerry, James Madison's Vice-President, who carved Massachusetts into election districts that favored his party. His opponents said the districts resembled wriggling salamanders, hence the term "gerrymandering." **See:** Reapportionment, Redistricting.

**GOVERNOR OF CALIFORNIA:** The chief executive of our state government. Because of California's prominence, the governor is also one of the most influential people in national politics. The state constitution requires a candidate for governor to be: 1) a citizen of the United States; 2) qualified to vote; 3) a resident of the state for at least 5 years immediately preceding the election. A governor has many titles, including: 1) Leader of his or her political party; 2) Ceremonial leader of the state; 3) Commander-in-chief; 4) Legislative leader.

**GOVERNOR'S CABINET:** An advisory group that provides the chief executive with a comprehensive overview of the state operations and helps with the policy making and long-term planning for California.

**GRANDFATHER CLAUSE:** Exempts existing persons or activities from provisions of an act.

**GRAND JURY:** A grand jury is a group of 19 citizens (23 in Los Angeles) that exists in each county. A grand jury can return indictments and investigates county government. **See:** Indictment.

**GRANT-IN-AID:** The federal government gives money to state and local governments through grant-in-aid. The money will always come with restrictions on how it is to be spent. **See:** Block Grant, Categorical Grant, Matching Funds, Revenue Sharing.

**GREEN PARTY:** California's newest political party whose main emphasis is in the area of environmental issues.

**GROSS NATIONAL PRODUCT (GNP):** This is the total output of goods and services in the national economy during a one year period.

**GUBERNATORIAL:** An adjective derived from the word governor that refers to anything that has to do with the office of governor.

**HABEAS CORPUS, WRIT OF:** A court order that requires that a jailed person must be brought before a judge for a determination of legal or illegal detention.

**HIGHWAY'S ACT (1984):** Reduced the amount of money available to states that allowed those under 21 years of age to legally consume alcoholic beverages.

**HOME RULE AMENDMENT (1911):** An amendment past by the state legislature which allowed for the creation of chartered counties. **See:** Charter Counties.

**HOUSE:** Legislative body, either the Assembly or Senate in California, not limited solely, as in Washington, D.C., to the lower house.

**IDEOLOGY:** A consistent political point of view on diverse topics. An ideological person is known as an ideologue.

**IMPEACHMENT:** Not to be confused with recall. Recall is initiated by the voters for any reason. Impeachment is conducted by the state legislature to remove an official from office for misconduct.

**IMPORTS:** Include all items produced in foreign countries that are purchased by Americans. **See:** Exports.

**INCORPORATION:** In reference to local government, the act of a community voting to become a city. The idea behind incorporation is to increase or maintain local control. The opposite of incorporation is disincorporation, a rare event in which a city dissolves its municipality.

**INCUMBENT:** This is the current officeholder.

**INDEXING:** The periodic adjustment of income tax brackets to eliminate the effects of inflation.

**INDICTMENT:** Charges filed against an individual if a grand jury, after a thorough investigation, believes that there is sufficient evidence of a crime. **See:** Grand Jury.

**INFRACTION:** The least serious type of crime - i.e, traffic ticket. **See:** Misdemeanor, Felony.

**INFRASTRUCTURE:** A basic strucure or foundation from which the very city or county itself is build; this includes the roadway, bridges, tunnels and mass transit facilities.

**INITIATIVE (DIRECT):** A process by which the people draft a proposal or constitutional amendment and acquire enough voter signatures to place the issue on the ballot where' it will be decided by all California voters. **See:** Direct Democracy.

**INTEREST GROUP:** An organized segment of voters that feel a certain way about a particular subject. Their objective is to have public policy embrace their goals and ideas. **See:** Private Agenda, PACs.

**JOHNSON, HIRAM:** The 23rd governor of California (1911-1917). He was a Progressive Republican whose political reforms included the initiative, recall, referendum, direct primary, nonpartisan city and county elections and a civil service system. **See:** Progressives.

**JOINT COMMITTEE:** A committee composed of members of both houses of a legislature.

**JUDGMENT:** The amount of money or non-monetary compensation awarded by the judge or jury to the prevailing party in a court case.

**JUDICIAL BRANCH:** In California, made up of the four court levels that interpret and apply California's laws (made by the state legislature and the governor) and our state constitution. The four court levels are: 1) Municipal and Justice Courts; 2) Superior Courts; 3) Court of Appeals; 4) Supreme Court.

**JUDICIAL COUNCIL:** A hard working group that has the responsibility to constantly improve the fairness and efficiency of our entire state court system.

**JUDICIAL REVIEW:** The power of a court to declare unconstitutional, after a complete review, any law passed by the legislature, or any action taken by the executive branch, that it deems to be in violation of the state or U.S. Constitution.

**JUDICIAL SYSTEM:** A state-run governmental activity to administer justice under the law.

**JURY TRIAL:** The process (in a criminal case) by which a group of 12 men and women have the task of determining whether the accused is innocent or guilty of the charges. In civil cases, the number of jury members is reduced to eight or less. **See:** Grand Jury, Civil Law Cases, Criminal Law Cases.

**JUSTICE COURT:** The lower court for criminal and civil action in areas where the population is 40,000 or less. The justice court has jurisdiction in most civil cases where the amount in question is $25,000 or less. **Compare:** Municipal Court.

**JUVENILE:** A person under the age of 18 who is treated differently in our legal system.

**LAW:** A rule of conduct determined by the people through their elected representatives, or by direct vote.

**LAW OF CHANGE:** The concept that change is always taking place; although on a day-to-day basis it may not be observable.

**LEAGUE OF WOMEN VOTERS:** A non-profit, nonpartisan volunteer group that educates voters as to issues and public problems. It is one of the few interest groups that presents its analysis to the general public in a straightforward, impartial manner. **See:** Interest Group.

**LEGISLATIVE ADVOCATE:** An individual engaged to present the views of a group or organization to legislators, and required by law to register with, and be certified by, the joint Rules Committee. More commonly referred to as a "lobbyist."

**LEGISLATIVE ANALYST:** Appointed by, and director of, the Joint Legislative Budget Committee. Analyzes the Governor's Budget and recommends any needed changes to the Legislature.

**LEGISLATIVE COUNSEL:** The chief legal counsel for the legislature, who is selected at the beginning of each session with the agreement of both houses.

**LEGISLATURE:** The arm of state government whose elected members represent the constituents in their home district, that makes new laws, oversees the implementation of laws through government bureaucracies and helps individuals with particular problems associated with government. The California legislature is composed of the 80 member Assembly, and the 40 member Senate. **Compare:** Assembly; Senate; Constituents; Lawmaking; Ombudsman; Oversight, Representation.

**LIBERAL:** A person or philosophy considered broad-minded and tolerant, favoring civil liberties, democratic reforms and the use of public resources to promote social progress. **See:** Conservative.

**LIEUTENANT GOVERNOR:** Independently elected, the Lieutenant Governor, despite his or her title, has very few significant duties in the State. Is an ex officio member of several boards and commissions and has gubernatorial powers if the governor is incapacitated, out of the state or there is a vacancy in the office.

**LINE ITEM VETO:** The power given to the governor allowing him or her to eliminate specific items and amounts in the state budget that are not to the governor's liking. **See:** Veto, Pocket Veto.

**LOBBYIST:** A person, representing a special interest group, who engages in influencing the introduction of legislation and the votes taken on bills in the legislature. **See:** Legislative Advocate.

**LOCAL AGENCY FORMATION COMMISSION (LAFCO):** The five member commission that defines the exact boundary lines of counties and cities.

**LOCAL AUTONOMY:** The authority of the local government to act independently, in most decisions, without the consent or control of the state. A common feature of county government. **See:** County.

**LOCAL CONTROL:** The process by which teachers and administrators are hired by the local board of education.

**LOWER HOUSE:** The Assembly.

**LONG BALLOT:** A ballot that includes many offices, items and initiatives to be decided upon by the voters. California uses a long ballot.

**MAJORITY VOTE:** A vote in which one candidate receives more than 50% of the vote.

**MANDAMUS, WRIT OF:** An order from a court that commands a public official to perform one of his or her official duties.

**MAQUILADORAS:** The name given to assembly and manufacturing plants in Mexico that do production work for American firms.

**MATCHING FUNDS:** Federal funds given to a state or local government which must be matched by that government body or they will not be granted. **See:** Grant-in-Aid.

**MAYOR:** The chief executive officer of a city. There are two types of mayoral systems: A strong mayor system, which has an independently elected mayor, and a weak mayor system, which has a mayor selected from among the city council members to carry out their programs.

**MISDEMEANOR:** A criminal offense (for example, disturbing the peace) that is less serious than a felony and that carries a maximum penalty of 1 year in the county jail.

**MISSION:** Spanish-style adobe type buildings with high arches, long corridors and red tile roofs that usually surround a courtyard. Besides being religious centers, missions were used as vocational centers for the native Indians. The first mission was established in San Diego (1769).

**MUNICIPAL COURT:** The lower court for criminal and civil action in areas of over 40,000 in population. The municipal court has jurisdiction in most civil cases where the amount in question is $25,000 or less. **Compare:** Justice Court.

**NONPARTISAN PRIMARY:** A primary election to nominate a candidate for an office to which no political party may legally nominate a candidate. These offices include: 1) Judges; 2) School board members, county and municipal offices; 3) The State Superintendent of Public Instruction. **See:** Primary Election.

**OFFICE-BLOCK BALLOT:** An election ballot that groups candidates by office sought, not by political party. This type of ballot is used in California and is one of the main reasons why we have people voting for different political parties for different offices (Ticket Splitting). **See:** Party-Column Ballot.

**OPEN PRIMARY:** A primary in which voters can decide when they arrive at the polls which party ballot they want. **See:** Closed Primary.

**OPEN-SEAT RACE:** An election in which none of the candidates is the incumbent for that particular office. **See:** Incumbent.

**ORDER OF SUCCESSION (FOR GOVERNOR):** The order of who assumes the governor's office in the event of death, resignation, removal or disability. The order is: 1) Lieutenant Governor, 2) President pro Tempore of the Senate; 3) Speaker of the Assembly; 4) Secretary of State; 5) Attorney General; 6) Treasurer, 7) Controller.

**ORDINANCES:** A law set forth by a governmental authority; for example a municipal regulation.

**OVERSIGHT COMMITTEES:** Committees within the legislature that act as watchdogs to make sure legislation or programs that have been passed by the legislature are being carried out properly by the employees of the executive branch. They also review the efficiency of programs to see if they can be accomplished more economically.

**PACS (POLITICAL ACTION COMMITTEES):** Use corporate, or union, resources to raise and distribute money to political campaigns supported by persons in corporations or in unions. **See:** Interest Group; Federal Election Commission; Fair Political Practices Commission.

**PARDON:** The governor's power to release a convicted criminal from the legal consequences of the crime. **Compare:** Clemency, Reprieve.

**PARTISAN:** This term has two meanings: formal registration in a political party and/or a sense of psychological identification with it.

**PARTY-COLUMN BALLOT:** A ballot, not used in California, that groups the candidates party-by-party instead of by the office being pursued. The top of the ballot has a box that, if marked by the voter, will cast a vote for all the candidates in one party for all the offices on the ballot. **See:** Office-Block Ballot.

**PATRONAGE:** A government job that is rewarded to a person for work that person did for a political candidate or party.

**PER DIEM ("per day"):** Daily expense money rendered legislators and their personnel.

**PERSONAL PROPERTY:** Includes all property other than land and buildings. **See:** Real Property.

**PETITION:** Formal request submitted by an individual, or group of individuals, to the Legislature.

**PLAINTIFF:** The party filing a civil action in court or the state filing a case in a criminal action. **Compare:** Defendant.

**PLEA BARGAINING:** The practice of pleading guilty to a reduced charge or sentence rather than standing trial on a more serious charge.

**PLURAL EXECUTIVE:** Refers to the fact that in California, not only is the chief executive (the governor) elected by the people, but so are other state executive officers, such as the lieutenant governor, secretary of state, the attorney general and the controller.

**PLURALITY:** The term used to describe a vote in which a candidate receives more votes than any other candidate but does not receive at least half of the votes. **See:** Majority Vote.

**POCKET VETO:** A term which really means that a governor fails to take any action on pending legislation after the legislature has adjourned. The constitutional revision of 1966 (extending time for legislative sessions) and the legislative reorganization of 1972 (continuous two-year session) effectively eliminated the pocket veto. **See:** Veto, Line Item Veto.

**POINT OF ORDER:** Motion calling attention to a breach of order or of rules.

**POINT OF PERSONAL PRIVILEGE:** Statement by a member of the Legislature that his or her character or purposes have been impugned, and his or-her refudiation of charges alleged to have been made.

**POLICE POWER:** The main power reserved for the states, by the federal government. It allows the state to take action to protect the public health, safety, morals and welfare of its citizens. **See:** Concurrent Power, Tenth Amendment.

**POLITICAL PARTY:** Most generally, an organization that puts forward candidates for public offices on the basis of shared general views as to political philosophy and solutions to current issues. Although many political scientists think that strong political parties are important for effective representative democracy, California political parties are weak. **Compare:** Linkage, Representative Democracy, Interest Groups, Interest Groups Versus, Political Parties.

**POLITICAL REFORM ACT (PROPOSITION 9):** Instituted to oversee more than 100,000 candidates for state and local government, their campaign funds and the activities of lobbyists. Also guarantees that voter ballot pamphlets will be independent, useful documents. **See:** Fair Political Practices Commission.

**POLLS (POLLING PLACE):** The location within a precinct where the voting takes place. The most common polling places are schools, public buildings and private residences. Polling places can not be in bars or liquor stores.

**PRECINCT:** A geographical area made up of a group of voters, from a low of 60 to a high of approximately 600 voters, depending on the election and how the registrar of voters wants them grouped.

**PRESIDENT OF THE SENATE:** The Lieutenant Governor, by constitutional enactment, is also President of the Senate.

**PRESIDENT PRO TEMPORE (OF THE SENATE):** A member or the state senate who is elected by his or her fellow senators to preside over the state senate in the absence of the lieutenant governor. Is also Chairperson of the Rules Committee. The President pro Tempore is generally considered the most powerful official in the senate. **Compare:** Speaker.

**PRESIDENTIAL PRIMARY:** The direct election of delegates to the national party conventions who select nominees, at those conventions, for president and vice president of the United States.

**PRESIDIO:** A frontier fort, located at a strategic area, usually at the entrance to a port or pueblo. Early presidios were located at San Francisco and Monterey.

**PRIMARY ELECTION:** An election, held (in California) on the first Tuesday after the first Monday in June of even numbered years, to select the following: 1) A party's candidates for important state offices in a direct primary; 2) Nonpartisan county and judicial officials, county party officials and the State Superintendent of Public Instruction; 3) The delegates to the national convention, of each political party, that will choose the candidates for president and vice president of the United States. **See:** Direct Primary.

**PRIVATE AGENDA:** Specific objectives set by an interest group in order to help it accomplish a specific goal. **See:** Interest Group, PACs.

**PROBATION:** The act of suspending the sentence of a convicted offender and giving the offender freedom during an examination period.

**PRODUCTIVITY:** The ability to produce more goods and services per working hour.

**PROGRESSIVE:** A person who favors restriction on corporate influence in politics and expansion of citizens' participation in politics, while protecting the environment and improving working and living conditions. **See:** Progressive Party.

**PROGRESSIVE PARTY:** An early 20th century reform party that consisted of disgruntled Republicans who wanted state powers returned to the people. Hiram Johnson was the Progressive Governor (1911-1917) who introduced such reform measures as: the initiative, recall and referendum; the direct primary; nonpartisan city and county elections and a civil service system.

**PROGRESSIVE TAX:** A tax (such as the income tax) that provides that as a person's income increases, the tax rate (expressed as a percentage) also increases. Its opposite is a regressive tax. **See:** Regressive Tax.

**PROPOSITION 13:** An initiative measure known as the Jarvis-Gann Amendment, passed in June, 1978, which limited the amount of property taxes that could be collected by local governments in California to one percent of the property's assessed value.

**PROPOSITION:** A qualified ballot measure that is given a number from one of these sources: 1) referendum petition; 2) compulsory referendum; 3) direct initiative.

**PUEBLO:** A Cluster of adobe houses, usually including a church, that formed a town or small city. Among the first pueblos were San Jose (1777) and Los Angeles (1781).

**QUORUM:** The minimum number of legislative members that, as required by law, must be present for the legislative body to officially conduct business, either on the floor or in committee hearings.

**RANCHO:** A large parcel of land that was given to a family of prominence in early California to establish unfenced grazing areas for raising cattle.

**REAL PROPERTY:** Consists of the land and any improvements on the land. **See:** personal property.

**RECALL:** The procedure by which any California state elected official can be removed from office, before the completion of his or her term, by a majority vote. This procedure takes a great deal of time and effort. **See:** Direct Democracy.

**REDISTRICTING (REAPPORTIONMENT):** All federal, state and local legislative district lines must be redrawn after each U.S. Census to reflect any changes, with regards to population growth or decline, in a given district. **See:** Gerrymander.

**REFERENDUM (BY PETITION):** The process of suspending the implementation of a law passed by the legislature (with approval of the governor or over his veto) until it can be voted on by the electorate. **See:** Direct Democracy, Compulsory Referendum.

**REGION:** A large geographic unit that can include many cities and counties and cover a large portion.of a state. **See:** Regional Governance.

**REGIONAL GOVERNANCE:** The process of regional planning and policy making with the input from cities, counties and businesses within the region.

**REGISTERED VOTER:** An eligible voter who has filled out an affidavit of registration and delivered it to the county clerk's office or registrar of voters by the 29th day before an election. A four-day grace period is given for mail-in registration.

**REGRESSIVE TAX:** A tax that affects those the most that are the least able to pay. An example is the sales tax. **See:** Progressive Tax.

**REPRIEVE:** Allows the governor to postpone. a sentence of the court from being carried out. **Compare:** Pardon, Clemency.

**RESCIND:** Annulment of an action previously taken, resulting in the restoration of the status quo.

**RESOLUTION:** A vote on a matter that involves one house, or both the assembly and the senate, but does not require the governor's approval. The four types of resolutions are: 1) Constitutional Amendment; 2) Concurrent Resolution; 3) Joint Resolution; 4) House Resolution.

**REVENUE:** Almost any money received, usually in the form of taxes, by the government. **See:** Earmarked Funds.

**REVENUE BONDS:** A type of bond that is issued to finance a project that will eventually produce revenue. A Toll bridge is an example. The income that will be generated from the project is the guarantee for the bond. **See:** Bond, General Obligation Bonds.

**REVENUE SHARING:** A now defunct program in which the federal government would give large amounts of money to local governments with basically no strings attached as to how the money could be utilized.

**RULES:** Methods of procedure: **Joint** – rules governing the relationship between and affecting matters between the two houses; **Standing** – permanent rules adopted by each house, for the duration of the session; **Temporary** – practices usually adopted at the beginning of each session until Standing Rules are adopted; consisting generally of the Standing Rules of the preceding session.

**SCHMOOZE:** A term used by lobbyists to define the art of discussing business in a social atmosphere. **See:** Lobbyist.

**SCHOOL DISTRICT:** The largest categories of districts in California. Every segment of California is divided into school districts.

**SECRETARY OF STATE:** California's independently elected official record keeper of the acts of the Legislature and the various executive departments. He or she is also supervisor of all State elections.

**SECRETARY OF THE SENATE:** An officer of the Senate, elected by the members to direct the clerical staff, the preparation of daily printing and general publications and to be of assistance to the presiding officer in interpreting the rules.

**SELECT COMMITTEE:** State legislative policy committees whose structure is such that they only consider a limited amount of legislation. **See:** Standing Committee.

**SENATE:** The upper house of the state legislature whose 40 members, half of whom are elected or re-elected every two years to 4 year terms (two-term limit), come from districts apportioned on the basis of population. **Compare:** Assembly, Legislature.

**SEVERANCE TAX:** An extraction tax on such depletable natural resource as gas, oil, timber and coal.

**SILICON VALLEY:** An area south of Stanford University in Northern California that is generally considered the electronic and computer manufacturing center of the United States.

**SIN TAX:** Taxes on such things as alcoholic beverages and tobacco. They produce a great deal of revenue for the state. **See:** Progressive, Regressive Tax.

**SINGLE ISSUE INTEREST GROUP:** Organizations made up of people who have a particular interest in, one subject and will fight for their cause until it is settled. Pro-choice groups and pro-life groups are examples of single issue groups. **See:** Interest Group.

**SMALL CLAIMS COURT:** A division of the municipal court, small claims courts are for civil cases where the current maximum judgment is $5000. Neither party in a small claims action may be represented by an attorney.

**SPEAKER (OF THE ASSEMBLY):** The presiding officer of the state assembly and the leader of the majority party in that body, who is elected at the beginning of each session. **Compare:** Assembly Speaker Pro Tempore, President Pro Tempore.

**SPEAKER PRO TEMPORE ("for the time"):** Substitute presiding officer of the Assembly, taking the chair on request of the Speaker, or in the Speaker's absence; elected by the Assembly at the beginning of each session.

**SPECIAL ELECTION:** An election, usually called by the governor, to fill unexpired terms and to decide certain ballot measures. Special elections can also occur on the local level.

**SPECIAL SESSION:** A session of the legislature, called by the governor, to deal with urgent matters. **See:** General Session.

**SPENDERS:** The segment of the population (Age 65 and older) who are the retirees living on social security and pensions. They are considered positive contributors to the economy because they spend money and pay more than their fair share in sales taxes. **See:** Earners, Users.

**STANDING COMMITTEE:** State legislative committees that have a great deal of jurisdiction in forming legislation. **See:** Select Committee.

**STATE BAR ASSOCIATION:** The professional association that is authorized by the state constitution to admit candidates to practice law in California and to set ethical standards, discipline and expel attorneys.

**STATE BOARD OF EQUALIZATION:** The California state agency that collects state sales taxes from businesses that in turn collect taxes from the consumer at the point of purchase.

**STATE CENTRAL COMMITTEE:** Made of partisan office holders, nominees, appointees and other minor party officials. Although it is considered a statewide governing body, it does not represent the rank-and-file party member in California. **See:** Executive Committee.

**STATE FRANCHISE TAX BOARD:** The California state agency that collects state income taxes from individuals and corporations. **See:** Indexing.

**STATE OF THE STATE ADDRESS:** A speech by the governor at the beginning of each legislative session in January to inform the senate and the assembly as to the condition of the state, his or her legislative agenda and recommendations for the year.

**STATUTES:** Compilation of all enacted bills, chaptered by the Secretary of State in the order in which they became law, and prepared in book form by the State Printer.

**SUPERINTENDENT OF PUBLIC INSTRUCTION:** California's independently elected nonpartisan director of the State Department of Education. The policies of the Department of Education are actually made by the ten-member State Board of Education, which is appointed by the Governor. The Superintendent is the Secretary of the State Board of Education and is supposed to implement the rules and regulations it adopts. **See:** Plural Executive.

**SUPERIOR COURT:** A state court set up in each county that has original jurisdiction over the major criminal and civil cases arising in that county. There is at least one superior court in each county.

**SUPREME COURT:** Being the highest court in California, the Supreme Court decides cases that raise broad and basic questions concerning law and social policy, and issues rulings intended to govern how similar cases will be decided in the future. The Supreme Court in California is made up of seven justices.

**SWING VOTERS:** The individual voters who have not committed themselves to a particular political party, issue or candidate but, if presented with an appealing campaign message, may vote for that issue or candidate. **See:** Campaign Strategy.

**TENTH AMENDMENT:** The amendment to the U.S. Constitution that gives the states their individual powers. **See:** Police Power, Concurrent Power.

**THIRD HOUSE:** The name given to lobbyists because of their influence on legislation. **See:** Lobbyist.

**TICKET-SPLITTING:** This occurs when a voter, while voting, does not stick to a party line, but rather selects candidates from different parties for different offices. Hence, the voter splits the ticket, or ballot.

**TRADE ASSOCIATION:** Organizations that are made up of similar businesses for the promotion of their common interests. Examples of trade associations are the California Chamber of Commerce, the California Manufacture's Association and the California Retailer's Association. **See:** Interest Group.

**TREASURER:** California's independently elected custodian of State money. The Treasurer is responsible for the auctioning of state bonds.

**TREATY OF GUADALUPE HIDALGO:** Signed on February 2, 1848, it brought to an end to the war with Mexico. As a result, the California Republic became a part of the United States as did Texas, New Mexico and Arizona.

**TRIAL COURT:** Most cases originate in a trial court. This is the court where a trial takes place. The municipal, justice and superior courts are trial courts. **See:** Appellate Court.

**TURNOUT:** The number of people, usually expressed as a percentage, who vote in a particular election.

**U.S. CONGRESS - CALIFORNIA DELEGATION:** Made up of two U.S. Senators and 53 members to the U.S. House of Representatives. California has the largest contingent to the Congress.

**U.S. CONGRESSIONAL MEMBER:** The term used to address the a member of the U.S. House of Representatives. California has 53 members in the House of Representatives.

**U.S. SENATE:** Made up of 100 senators, two from each state. Each U.S. Senator must be at least 30 years of age and have been a U.S. citizen for nine years. A U.S. Senator serves a six year term.

**UNINCORPORATED AREA:** A section of a county that is not part of any city.

**UPPER HOUSE:** The Senate.

**URGENCY LAW:** A law to protect immediately the public peace, health or safety. These laws must pass the state legislature by a two-thirds vote, and they take effect immediately.

**URGENT BILL:** A bill that must take effect immediately after it is enacted. It requires a two-thirds vote of the legislature. **See:** Bill, Appropriation Bill.

**USERS:** The segment of the population (Under 18 years of age) that utilize most of the public services: education, child care and welfare. **See:** Earners, Spenders.

**USER FEES:** A charge for a public service, that is levied on those who use the service, to help pay for that service. Examples include fees to enter a city or county museum or to play golf on a county or city-run golf course.

**VETO:** The total rejection of any bill by the governor that can only be overridden by a two-thirds vote of both the State Assembly and State Senate. It is the biggest legislative weapon the governor holds. **See:** Line Item Veto, Pocket Veto.

**VOTER BALLOT PAMPHLET:** A booklet sent to each registered voter explaining propositions and ballot measures before the electorate.

**VOTER LIST:** The list of registered voters by name, address, party affiliation and, in California, phone number that is supplied, for a small charge, to precincts by the county registrar of voters. **See:** Campaign Strategy.

**VOTER PURGE:** The action of the registrar of voters reviewing the list of registered voters on a systematic basis and eliminating certain voters from their rolls. The usual reason for removal is the voter's failure to have voted in the last general election. California does not use a voter purge system.

**VOTER TARGETING:** The deliberate attempt on the part of a campaign to identify the precincts or election districts in which to consolidate its effort in order to win. **See:** Campaign Strategy.

**VOUCHER SYSTEM:** A proposed educational reform system where the state provides a voucher or scholarship worth $2500 to $3500 for each school-aged child, thereby allowing the parents to choose a public or private school.

**WATER DISTRICT:** A district organized to provide water to a large portion of a state. In California, the Metropolitan Water District (MWD) is the largest. **See:** District.

**WORKINGMEN'S PARTY:** An anti-railroad monopoly party that disapproved of the large numbers of unemployed Chinese workers left in the wake of the railroad construction period. Their proposed reform measures lead to the Second California State Constitution.

# Index

10th Amendment: 30

## A

Absentee Ballot: 43
Admission Day: 24
Air Quality: 9
   Air Quality Management District (AQMD): 9
Air Quality Management District (AQMD): 9, 131
Appellate Court: 108
Appropriation Bill: 98
Arraignment: 112
Assembly Speaker Pro Tempore: 96
Assembly, California: 95
   Assembly Speaker Pro Tempore: 96
   Majority Party Floor Leader: 96
   Minority Party Floor Leader: 96
   Speaker of the Assembly: 96
Association of Bay Area Governments (ABAG): 131
At-Large Elections: 43
Attorney General: 82
Auditor General: 100

## B

Bail: 113
Ballot Forms: 44
   Long Ballot: 44
   Office-Block Ballot: 44
   Party-Column Ballot: 44
Bear Flag Revolt: 21
Bicameral: 91
Bill: 91, 98
   Appropriation Bill: 98
   Urgent Bills: 98
Blanket Primary: 38
Block Grant: 31
Bonds: 146
   California's Bond Rating: 147
   General Obligation Bond: 146
   Revenue Bond: 146

Budget Process: 139
   Line Item Veto: 139
Business Challenge: 13
Business Climate: 146

## C

Cabrillo, Juan Rodriquez: 17
California Budget Crisis: 1
California Caucus: 30
California Chamber of Commerce: 62
California Flag: 21-22
California Missions: 20
California Supreme Court: 109, 115
California's Economy: 13
CAL-SPAN: 101
Campaign Laws: 69
   Fair Political Practices Commission: 69
   Federal Election Campaign Act: 69
   Proposition 34 (Limitations on Contributions): 70
Campaign Message: 68
Campaign Strategy: 68
Capital Punishment: 80
Categorical Grants: 31
Census: 5
Central Pacific Railroad: 25
   Southern Pacific Railroad: 29
Charter (Home Rule) City: 126
Cinco de Mayo: 20
Cities: 126
   Charter (Home Rule) City: 126
   City Council: 127
   City Manager: 127
   City Revenue: 127
   Council-Manager: 127
   General Law City: 126
   Incorporation: 126
   Local Agency Formation Commission (LAFCO): 126
   Mayor: 127
   Other City Administrators: 127
   Strong Mayor System: 127

# Index

Unincorporated Area: 126
Weak Mayor System: 127
City Council: 127
City Manager: 127
Civil Cases: 108, 113
Clemency: 80
Closed Primary: 38
Commission on Judicial
 Appointments: 111
Commission on Judicial Nominees: 111
Commission on Judicial
 Performance: 111
Community Colleges: 7-8
Commute: 80
Complaint: 113
Concurrent Powers: 30
Concurrent Resolution: 99
Conference Committees: 97
Confirmation: 94
Conservative: 65
Consolidated Elections: 41
Constitutional Amendment: 93, 99
 Fiscal Committees: 97
Constitutional Convention: 29
Council of Government (COGs): 130
 Association of Bay Area
  Governments (ABAG): 131
 Southern California Association of
  Government (SCAG): 131
Council-Manager: 127
Counties: 122
 Charter (Home Rule) Counties: 122
 County Board of Supervisors: 122
 County Expenditures: 125
 County Revenue: 122
 Functions of the County: 124
 General Law Counties: 122
 Other County Officials: 123
 Proposition 13: 123
County Board of Supervisors: 122
County Central Committee: 66
Court of Appeal: 109
Court Procedures: 112
 Civil Cases: 113
  Complaint: 113
 Criminal Cases: 112
  Arraignment: 112
  Bail: 113

Felonies: 113
Infractions: 113
Juvenile Offenders: 113
Misdemeanors: 113
Own Recognizance: 113
Plea Bargaining: 113
Probation: 113
Criminal Cases: 108, 112
Crocker, Charles: 25
Crowd Lobbying: 64
C-SPAN: 101

## D

*Daily File*: 100
*Daily History*: 100
*Daily Journal*: 100
Davis, Gray: 1
Defendant: 108
Defense Attorney: 115
Deficit: 139
Democrats: 64-65
Direct Democracy: 49
Direct Initiative: 49, 56
 Initiative Reform: 57
 Proposition: 57
Direct Primary: 38
District Attorney (D.A.): 115
District Elections: 43
Districts: 129
 School Districts: 129
 Water Districts: 130

## E

Early California History: 17
 Bear Flag Revolt: 21
 Cabrillo, Juan Rodriquez: 17
 California Flag: 21-22
 California Missions: 20
 California's Political/Historical
  Timeline: 18
 Cinco de Mayo: 20
 El Camino Real: 20
 Gold: 22
 Mexican Rule: 20
  Mexican Secularization Act: 20
 Native Americans: 17

# Index

Spain: 17
Statehood: 24
  Admission Day: 24
  Treaty of Guadalupe Hidalgo: 22
Earmarked Funds: 145
Economic Diversity: 14
El Camino Real: 20
Election Laws: 67
Endorsement: 68
Ethnic Diversity: 5, 12
Ex Officio: 84
Executive Branch: 77
  Administration of: 81
  Agencies: 82
  Governor's Cabinet: 81
  Governor: 77-78
  Order of Succession: 77
  Plural Executive: 77
Executive Committee: 66
Exports: 14

## F

Fair Political Practices
  Commission: 67, 69
Federal Election Campaign Act: 69
Federal Indian Gaming Regulatory
  Act: 27
Felonies: 113
*Final History*: 100
Fuel Cell Vehicles: 131

## G

General Election: 40
General Law City: 126
Gerrymandering: 93
Gold: 22
Government Fiscal Year: 139
Governor: 77-78
  Commander-in-Chief: 80
  Gubernatorial: 78
  Legislative Leader: 80
  Line Item Veto: 80
  Personal Staff: 82
  Pocket Veto: 81
  State of the State Address: 80
Governor's Cabinet: 81

Governors of the State of California: 87
Grand Jury: 116
  Indictment: 117
Grant-in-Aid: 31
Great Seal: 24
Gross Domestic Product (GDP): 14
Growth Projections: 3
  Regional Growth Projections: 4
Gubernatorial: 78

## H

Hearst, William Randolph: 25
High Technology: 3
Higher Education: 7-8
Highway Patrol: 116
Home Rule: 122
Hopkins, Mark: 25
House Resolution: 99
Housing: 10
Huntington, Collis P.: 25

## I

Impeachment: 54, 94
Imports: 14
Incorporation: 126
Incumbent: 32
Indexing: 141
Indian Casino Gambling: 70
Indictment: 117
Infractions: 113
Insurance Commissioner: 84
Interest Groups: 61
  Demographic Interest Groups: 62
  Lobbyist: 62
  Private Agendas: 61
  Single-Issue Interest Groups: 62
  Trade Associations: 62
    California Chamber of Commerce: 62

## J

Jobs: 2
Johnson, Hiram : 49
  Progressive Reforms: 51
Joint Committees: 97
Joint Resolution: 99

# Index

Judgment: 108
Judicial Council: 112
Judicial System: 107
  and the U.S. Supreme Court: 112
  Appellate Court: 108
  California Supreme Court: 109
  Citizens' Participation: 116
    Grand Jury: 116
    Jury Trial: 116
    Witness: 116
  Civil Cases: 108, 113
  Commission on Judicial
    Appointments: 111
  Commission on Judicial
    Nominees: 111
  Commission on Judicial
    Performance: 111
  Court of Appeal: 109
  Criminal Cases: 108, 112
  Defendant: 108
  Defense Attorney: 115
  District Attorney (D.A.): 115
  Judgment: 108
  Judicial Council: 112
  Peace Officers: 116
    Highway Patrol: 116
    Marshal: 116
    Police Officer: 116
    Sheriff: 116
    State Police: 116
  Plaintiff: 108
  Public Defender: 115
  Small Claims Court: 109
  Superior Court: 108
  Three-Level Court Structure: 108
  Trial Court: 108
Jury Trial: 116
Juvenile Offenders: 113

## K - L

K-12 Education: 6-7
L.A. County Board of Supervisors: 125
Landfills: 10
League of Women Voters: 65
Legislation, Types of: 98
  Bills: 98
    Appropriation Bill: 98
    Urgent Bills: 98
  Resolution: 99
Legislative Analyst: 100
Legislative Counsel: 100
*Legislative Index*: 100
Legislative Leader: 80
Legislature, California: 91
  Assembly: 95
  Bicameral: 91
  Committee System: 96
    Conference Committees: 97
    Fiscal Committees: 97
    Joint Committees: 97
    Rules Committees: 96
    Select or Special Committees: 97
    Standing Committees: 96
  Confirmation: 94
  Constitutional Amendment: 93
  General Session: 92
  Gerrymandering: 93
  Impeachment: 94
  Legislative Process: 91
    Bill: 91
    Veto Override: 92
  Legislative Staff: 100
    Auditor General: 100
    Legislative Analyst: 100
    Legislative Counsel: 100
  Media Coverage: 101
    CAL-SPAN: 101
    C-SPAN: 101
    Newspapers, State: 102
  Oversight Committees: 93
  Reapportionment: 92
  Requirements (for Election): 97
  Salary: 97
  Senate: 94
  Special Session: 92
  Term Limits (Proposition 140): 99
Liberal: 66
Lieutenant Governor: 82, 95
Line Item Veto: 80, 139
Lobbyist: 62
  Crowd Lobbying: 64
  Schmooze: 64
Local Agency Formation Commission
  (LAFCO): 126
Local Control: 143

# Index

Long Ballot: 44

## M

Majority Vote: 39
Mandates: 131
Marshal: 116
Marshall, James Wilson: 22
Matching Funds: 31
Mayor: 127
Metropolitan Water District (MWD): 130
Mexican Secularization Act: 20
Misdemeanors: 113

## N - O

Native Americans: 17
Nonpartisan Primary: 39
Office-Block Ballot: 44
Order of Succession: 77
Oversight Committees: 93
Own Recognizance: 113

## P

Pardon: 80
Party-Column Ballot: 44
Plaintiff: 108
Plea Bargaining: 113
Plural Executive: 77, 82
   Attorney General: 82
   Insurance Commissioner: 84
   Lieutenant Governor: 82
   Secretary of State: 83
   State Board of Equalization: 84
   State Controller: 83
   Superintendent of Public Instruction: 84
   Treasurer: 83
Pocket Veto: 81
Police Officer: 116
Police Power: 30
Political Action Committees (PACs): 68
Political Campaigns: 68
   Campaign Message: 68
   Campaign Strategy: 68
   Swing Voters: 69
   Voter List: 69
   Voter Targeting: 69

Political Parties: 64
   American Independent: 64
   County Central Committee: 66
   Democratic: 64
   Executive Committee: 66
   Green: 64
   Libertarian: 65
   Natural Law: 64
   Peace and Freedom: 64
   Reform: 64
   Republican: 65
   State Central Committee: 66
Political Reform Act: 67
Polling Palce (Poll): 43
Population: 2, 11, 33, 138
Precincts: 41
   Polling Palce (Poll): 43
Presidential Primary: 40
Primary Elections: 38
   Blanket Primary: 38
   Closed Primary: 38
   Direct Primary: 38
   Nonpartisan Primary: 39
     Majority Vote: 39
   Presidential Primary: 40
Prisons: 9, 145
Probation: 113
Productivity: 12
Progressive: 49
Progressive Tax: 142
Progressives: 29
Proposition: 57
Proposition 13: 123
Proposition 140 (Term Limits): 99
Proposition 34 (Limitations on Contributions): 70
Proposition 98: 140
Public Defender: 115

## R

Railroads: 25
   Central Pacific Railroad: 25
   Crocker, Charles: 25
   Hearst, William Randolph: 25
   Hopkins, Mark: 25
   Huntington, Collis P.: 25
   Pacific Railroad Bill: 25

# Index

Stanford, Leland: 25
Ranchos: 21
Reaportionment: 92
Recall: 49, 52
   Impeachment: 54
   Recall Petition: 52
Redistricting (Reapportionment): 33
Redistricting Lawsuit: 125
Referendum: 49, 55
   Compulsory Referendum: 56
Region: 130
Regional Governance: 130
   Council of Government (COGs): 130
   Region: 130
Regional Growth Projections: 4
Regressive Tax: 142
Reprieve: 80
Republicans: 65
Resolution: 98-99
   Concurrent Resolution: 99
   Constitutional Amendmen: 99
   House Resolution: 99
   Joint Resolution: 99
Rules Committees: 96

## S

Schmooze: 64
School Districts: 129
School Enrollment Trends: 7
Schwarzenegger, Arnold: 1, 77
Second State Constitution: 29
Secretary of State: 56, 83
Select or Special Committees: 97
*Semifinal History*: 100
Senate President Pro Tempore: 95
Senate Rules Committee: 95
Senate, California: 94
   Lieutenant Governor: 95
   Majority and Minority Floor Leaders: 95
   Senate President Pro Tempore: 95
   Senate Rules Committee: 95
Sheriff: 116
Sin Taxes: 142
Single-Issue Interest Groups: 62
Small Claims Court: 109
Southern California Association of Government (SCAG): 131

Southern Pacific Railroad: 29
Speaker of the Assembly: 96
Special Election: 41
Standing Committees: 96
Stanford, Leland: 25
State Bar of California: 114
State Board of Equalization: 84, 141
   Ex Officio: 84
State Budget Crisis: 137
   Budget Problems: 140
   Deficit: 139
   Government Fiscal Year: 139
   Proposition 98: 140
   State Budget: 139
State Central Committee: 66
State Controller: 83
State Franchise Tax Board : 140
State of the State Address: 80
State Police: 116
State Powers: 30
   10th Amendment: 30
   Concurrent Powers: 30
   Police Power: 30
State Spending 2003: 144
State Taxes, Types of: 140
   Indexing: 141
   Progressive Tax: 142
   Regressive Tax: 142
   Sin Taxes: 142
   State Board of Equalization: 141
   State Franchise Tax Board : 140
   State Taxes 2003-2004: 141
   Where Taxes Go: 143
      Earmarked Funds: 145
      State Spending 2003: 144
Statehood: 24
   Admission Day: 24
Strong Mayor System: 127
Superintendent of Public Instruction: 84
Superior Court: 108
Sutter, John: 22
Swing Voters: 69

## T

Three Strikes Law: 114
Ticket-Splitting: 65
Trade Associations: 62

# Index

Transportation: 9
Treaty of Guadalupe Hidalgo: 22
Trial Court: 108

## U

U.S. Congress: 32
   U.S. House of Representatives: 29, 32
   U.S. Senate: 29, 32
U.S. Supreme Court: 112
UC, CSU: 7-8
Unincorporated Area: 126
Urgent Bills: 98

## V

Veto: 80
   Line Item Veto: 80
   Pocket Veto: 81
Veto Override (Legislative): 92
Voter List: 69
Voter Purge: 44
Voter Targeting: 69
Voting: 37, 57
   Absentee Ballot: 43
   Registered Voter: 37
   Voter Ballot Pamphlet: 57
   Voter Purge: 44
   Voters' Time Schedule: 42
   Who Votes?: 40

## W

Waste Management: 10
   Landfills: 10
Water: 10
Water Districts: 130
   Metropolitan Water District (MWD): 130
Weak Mayor System: 127
*Weekly History*: 100
Welfare: 31
Witness: 116
Workingman's Party: 29
   Second State Constitution: 29